Empowering S Future

Empowering Students for the Future: Using the Right Questions to Teach the Value of Passion, Success, and Failure arms educators with the tools to teach what we all wish we had learned in school. You will discover how to help your students think deeper, redefine failure, and authentically create their definition of success.

Author Eric Yuhasz offers a variety of practical ideas throughout, including rapid-fire questions and a bowl meeting structure to help students find their passions; activities to help students address negativity from social media plus negative, self-inflicted mantras they may unconsciously be following; a chart that enables students to see their progress toward achieving their definition of success; tips for discussing value, sacrifice, self-discipline, motivation, and the tyranny of low expectations; plus ideas for helping students embrace failure as a stepping stone toward learning and triumph. With clear strategies in each chapter, this unique book will show you how your learners can truly map out a happier, healthier, more successful future.

Eric Yuhasz's goal is to build an army of successful students. He is an award-winning, public-school teacher, magician and speaker. After years of teaching, he still loves educating and has crafted a way to burst out of the borders of his classroom. By merging his classroom message with magic, he now shares his motivational message traveling from coast to coast.

Empowering Students for the Future

Using the Right Questions to Teach the Value of Passion, Success, and Failure

Eric Yuhasz

Routledge
Taylor & Francis Group

NEW YORK AND LONDON

Designed cover image: Getty images

First published 2023
by Routledge
605 Third Avenue, New York, NY 10158

and by Routledge
4 Park Square, Milton Park, Abingdon, Oxon, OX14 4RN

Routledge is an imprint of the Taylor & Francis Group, an informa business

ISBN: 978-1-032-44917-3 (hbk)
ISBN: 978-1-032-44804-6 (pbk)
ISBN: 978-1-003-37449-7 (ebk)

DOI: 10.4324/9781003374497

Typeset in Palatino
by SPi Technologies India Pvt Ltd (Straive)

Contents

Meet the Author

Eric Yuhasz's goal is to build an army of successful students. He is an award-winning, public-school teacher, magician and speaker. After more than two decades as an educator, he still loves teaching and has crafted a way to burst out of the borders of his classroom. By merging his life and classroom message with magic, he now gets to travel from coast to coast sharing his motivational magic with schools, colleges, and businesses. After a stint as a news reporter, Eric earned a Master's degree in math and science education from the University of Central Florida where he lives in Orlando. Just for kicks, he loves playing beach volleyball and flying small two-seater airplanes.

Preface

The following is an unsolicited email from a former student. It not only gives you an insight into my passion and purpose, but it also spotlights the power of asking the right reflection questions. These questions lead the learners through a reflective process and can empower them to live happier, healthier, more successful lives.

Hi Mr. Yuhasz,

It's Lydia. I wanted to say thank you for everything you've done for me. You are such a great teacher and I am so grateful for the past two years I got to spend in your classroom. You taught me so much. You are such a great engineering teacher but I'm even more thankful for the things you taught me about life, hard work, and success. Every bowl talk, discussion after class, random lecture in the middle of class, or lunch I got to spend in your class are moments I am so appreciative of and will never forget.

You taught me more than any other teacher ever has and you always go above and beyond because you want us to succeed. You are one of the best teachers I've ever had and the amount of effort you put in just to help us succeed is incredible and shows how much you truly care. I wanted to tell you to always keep doing this and teaching the way you are because even if sometimes it's discouraging and it feels like no one's listening, there is always at least one kid you are reaching. You are going to have a big impact on their lives.

I know that even last year there was a big group of us who you impacted and who left your class every day having learned something new. You have taught me how to work hard, live up to my own standards and not do the bare minimum, knowing what success means to me, and how I'm gonna achieve that every day. I wish I could come back to your class every day because I know I would keep learning new things and always have your support as a teacher. You stood out as a teacher because you cared about not just grades, but us actually learning. Not just our work but our lives. Not just each day in the classroom but you invested in our future.

I thank you for that and I know every new student from now on is so lucky to be in your class. I hope you have a great year this year even without your favorite class ever :). Also your magic shows were always great and really fun to watch.

P.S. I want a signed copy of your book when it's finished.

Sincerely, Lydia J.

(She most definitely will get a signed copy.)

So why do I share this self-congratulatory-sounding message? Not as a form of bragging, but to emphasize the value of teaching as it relates to encouraging young people (and those older, too) to think about success. Not just about earning a pile of money, but about how they define success. To someone who grew up wondering where their next meal was coming from, that may mean earning enough money to never look at an empty pantry again. But to someone else, it may mean painting colorful images of the past to illuminate and interpret the historical events that tie us together. It could mean becoming a motivational speaker to encourage others to reach for the stars and not let the natural negativity of naysayers doom them to a life of settling for second-best, or, giving up just because something has never been done before. It may mean doing what I do: teaching adolescents in the prime of their life to think about what they really want to do, define what matters to them, and then carve out a path toward their future.

The reason I feel so passionate about doing what I do stems from an experience I had while still in high school. Growing up in a town of less than ten thousand meant it was common to have the same teacher for more than one academic year. Thus, for three of my four years in high school, I had the same math teacher. About three-fourths of the way through my year in trigonometry class, this teacher pulled me aside and said, "Eric, I have never had someone have this high an average in this class."

As you can imagine, that felt pretty good. Yet to this day, I wish she would have gone a step further and encouraged me to think about math as a career—given me some suggestions about further training, colleges where I might have developed this gift into something more—and planted the idea in my mind that this could be a field that offered me a future.

That's where I think education falls short too often. I know teachers care about their students and want to help them fulfill their dreams; I work alongside dozens of them every day. But, too often, education follows an Industrial Age model aimed at equipping people with knowledge rather than teaching them how to use it nimbly to adapt to a world changing so fast that two decades from now we will look back on 2023 as "the good old days."

This is why I seek to inspire my students to think about what they hope to do one day and how they can use their gifts to not just enrich themselves, but benefit others around them. To share an example from my classroom where I tried to support a student's passion: one year, I noticed a student who was exceptional at art. I pulled her aside and offered to pay her to draw me a picture of me performing magic, which is a hobby and a vocation. You should have seen her face light up when I offered her this deal! I have no idea where she will take her talent, but I think she will go far. I am doing my best here to encourage students like her in their passions.

Whether you are a teacher, a professor, or a parent who is homeschooling a couple youngsters, I hope you will seek to do the same. Success starts with reflecting about it.

1

How Can We Evolve Education to Create More Successful Students?

If you are searching for answers, you have come to the wrong place. Only you can provide the answers. This book is just a conduit to the right questions. Unfortunately, most of the questions you have been asked thus far in life have been the wrong ones. Let's remedy that now. It is never too late to start asking yourself the right questions to cultivate success in your own life. Where you are in your personal journey determines how easily these ideas can blossom. As with so many things in life, the sooner a person begins to reflect on the right ideas and concepts, the easier these can be integrated to truly redirect that person's life. Therefore, I have chosen to teach them to my students.

What proceeds are ideas that are appropriate to all, but these lessons are especially applicable to teachers. Because of this, I will present how I integrate thought-provoking questions and discussions in my classroom to nurture students' thinking about success. Thus, at first glance, it appears I am targeting teachers and students. With further examination though, I am targeting you: the reader. The person who wants to start a ripple of personal, student, or global change. The change I am referring to is a paradigm shift in the way we think about success. It is deconstructing what has always been taught or—more aptly put—what has not been taught. Also, it dives into our prior

DOI: 10.4324/9781003374497-1

knowledge and preconceived notions around the topic of success. In its essence, the change occurs by us authentically defining what success means. That is something not currently being taught in most schools.

Regrets come from the moments in life when we could have added value to ourselves but failed to do so. If that statement is even partially true, then what happens when the one institution in charge of adding value to our lives misses the mark? What happens when we trust that institution to provide for us the value needed to succeed in life, but we are left to our own devices to fill in the gaps? What happens when traditional education has failed us?

You don't have to look far for the answers to those previous questions. A survey conducted in 2018 points toward the average American only using 37% of what they learned in school. This survey revealed Americans' desire to learn other more applicable topics in school, such as time management, how to manage emotional/mental wellbeing, and understanding credit [1].

Do you agree with that survey? Try conducting a quick inventory of what you learned in school. My guess is you could rattle off item after item of topics you learned about that have no particular value to your life outside of school. Here is just one example of something I had to learn in school that has no relevance to my life whatsoever.

Whan that Aprille with his shoures soote,
The droghte of March hath perced to the roote,
And bathed every veyne in swich licóur
Of which vertú engendred is the flour ...[2]

That is part of the prologue to *The Canterbury Tales*, the legendary English literature collection of twenty-four stories penned between 1387 and 1400. Yes, I had to memorize that in school and for some unearthly reason I still remember it. As your brain continues to marinate over the topic of items you learned but never used again, it is an easy transition to contemplate the things you wish you had learned. In his book, *Future Wise: Educating Our Children for a Changing World*, former Harvard University education professor Dr. David Perkins dives into this topic. He writes, "Just as educators are pushing students to build a huge reservoir of knowledge, they are also focused on having students master material, sometimes at the expense of relevance [3]."

Sorting Through Content

I am willing to bet you have already come to that same conclusion about education. You have sorted through what was relevant and what was not and had to somehow learn the more valuable content through living. The cost of learning through living can be very high, whether the currency is time, money, or even happiness.

If you and I can agree what we learned—or more importantly, what we didn't learn—in school has impacted our lives, then we are on a level playing ground. Now, we have the foundation to move forward, together. Before we go any further, it is imperative to know this book is not about destroying the education system. It is about helping education evolve. It is about redefining education and filling those learning gaps that have been plaguing Americans for decades. It is about adding value to the learner's life that has been absent from most traditional school settings. Before we discover how this content can and will change the way learners view life, and will propel them to living a greater, more success-filled life, there is another short self-assessment I would like you to conduct.

At first glance, this is going to seem unrelated, but I assure you it most definitely is connected. Think of the five closest people in your life. How many of them would you say have a growth mindset? This means they are always striving for improvement while not allowing the emotions of the past to dictate their future. Are you lucky enough to have one among those five who possess such a mindset? If we are the summation of our five closest friends, then do you have a growth mindset?

Please understand I am not casting judgment on you or your friends. It is not your fault or theirs. Instead, I circle back to the education system, which provides a very rigid, short-term view of success. If students begin to think outside the box in a class-room, they are typically met with opposition via the instructor. In describing her road to success and becoming the billionaire creator of the company Spanx, Sara Blakely (almost word for word) reiterates this concept. She describes how, despite sixteen years of schooling, she never learned how to think. Being an edu-cator, recognizing this fact sends tremors through my soul [4].

Teaching at an arts academy, the physical flexibility of the students in dance class always amazes me. There is no way they could succeed in that field without dedicated, determined, devoted routines of stretching and dance practice five, six, or even seven days a week. This is how they are able to perform at such a high level with such flexibility. For years, these students have been taught to increase their flexibility.

How great would it be if we taught them how to increase their mental flexibility in the same way? With the right instruc-tion from you, students can discipline themselves to do just that. Why not instruct students at an early age how to be flexible of mind to reduce the likelihood of sustaining lifelong emotional injuries and direct them to a deeper understanding of success, all at the same time?

Helping Education Evolve

Using such a method means not only can we begin to help edu-cation evolve, but we can also be among rare individuals in our learners' lives who provide them with a growth mindset. And not only provide them with an example but teach them how to achieve it. Therein lies the genesis of this book: a step-by-step process of walking a learner through being reflective, men-tally flexible, and forward thinking. These are all skills that are imperative to creating a successful future in a rapidly changing world.

Although the signs of success and traits needed to obtain success are somewhat universal, success is a specialized, unique, exciting journey for the individual. This is why answering the question: "What is your definition of success?" poses such a challenge. Success cannot be genuinely defined until a person conducts a thorough self-audit.

There is one universal truth that must be accepted prior to any change, whether personal, classroom, or global. *There is no way to have authentic, life-changing, long lasting and self-improving change without first enduring a soul-searching, gut-wrenching self-reflection.* Please absorb that statement. I should warn you, acceptance of it comes with a cost. For you, personally, it means revisiting your past mistakes, regrets, and moments you deem as failures. If you are an educator, it comes at the cost of investing your heart into these concepts and surrendering class time. On both accounts, the rewards are priceless and 100% worth going down those dark alleyways of your past or sacrificing a smidge of time devoted to your subject area. Those rewards only come amidst the iterative process of reflection.

"Mirror, mirror, on the wall ..."

Reflection is such a fickle word. From birth we associate it with a mirror, much as the queen in *Snow White* did. For most of us that means a quick glance, coupled with a few adjustments, and we are off for the day. But, to be a little bit cheesy in my wording, the deeper you reflect over the word reflection, the more it will take on new life.

To examine further, I came to education as a second career. I will reveal the full story of my past later, but for now, let's hop into this midstride. I worked as a news reporter. Yes, I was the person standing out in the rain talking about a traffic accident. Think about what "reflect" means in that field: a quick glance in the side mirror of your vehicle before going live from the field, or a slightly longer glance in the mirror to make sure you look attractive to the audience. In such a fast-paced arena, "reflection" meant: how did I look? Once I finished a story, I was off to the next, with little time to reflect on the finished product.

When I landed in education, reflection took on a whole new meaning. As I progressed through the additional coursework needed to make the transition to teaching, that word kept popping up repeatedly. Reflect on this. Reflect on that. I thought to myself, "Is this all teachers do? Reflect? That is so easy." It wasn't until I went through the process of getting my National Board Certification as a teacher that my understanding of the word "reflect" began to more fully develop.

I worked with the professor who literally wrote the book on how to pass the National Board Certification test. She sat with me and evaluated a few recorded teaching lessons I was going to submit as part of the application process. In the process, she kept pausing the video and asking me, "Well, why did you do that?" Each moment she asked that question, she wanted me to crack open the shell of my psyche and reveal my line of thinking. The majority of the time she pointed out the good instinctive things I did, which I did not realize I was doing. By deeply analyzing not just the good and the bad moments, but the "why" behind those moments, she helped to reinforce good teaching practices and release poor ones.

What Works

From that moment on, the true definition of reflection became apparent to me. It was more than a way of facing the goods, the bads, and the uglies. It was making a conscious effort to enhance the goods, eliminate the bads, and beautify the uglies. Essentially, it was a matter of routinely asking:

1. What worked well?
2. What didn't work well?
3. What role did I play in things going well or poorly?
4. What would I do differently in the future?

As simplistic as these questions might appear, when was the last time you reflected on something and posed such questions to yourself? The journey to changing who we are and how we perform starts with a deeper understanding of who we are to begin with and what got us here. The above four questions just scratch the surface of the kind of reflection that is needed to produce a life that has endless possibilities. What decisions, actions, traumas, and events formed the way we think, feel, and live? How have we anchored current emotions to past events that we now carry with us into the future?

The only way we can understand ourselves is if we take the time to sort out the topic we claim to know best: self. No, I am not trying to talk in circles. We must rip back the curtain and admit who we are, how we got here, and then where we want to go. The right questions asked of ourselves, coupled with thorough reflection, can start us all on the path to a truly fulfilled life.

With age, we experience more of those actions, traumas, and events that can cause resonating emotions in our lives. It is the rigidity of our minds, which often perpetuates those thoughts and feelings from our past, that hinders us from grasping success in the present and the future. Deeply reflecting on who we are, how we got here, and who we want to be is a way of increasing our mind's range of motion. It is increasing our flexibility of thinking so when the challenges of life roll our way, we are prepared to bend and not break. Imagine catching minds at an earlier age when they are more pliable. Imagine catching minds before the challenges of life detrimentally impact them. Imagine preparing those minds in such a way that the challenges of life are viewed less like catastrophes and more like catalysts to a better life.

The value contained in this book is outlined in a way that means teachers can easily share this information. However, when I use the term "teachers," it is in the sense of someone educating someone else. That can come in the form of teacher-to-student, parent-to-child, friend-to-friend, or any other form of facilitator of knowledge-and-learner. It might just mean you teaching yourself. Since I have been a teacher for over two decades, this information has been battle-tested in the classroom. I am disseminating it to you in the way I teach it to my students. Yet, you only need modest effort to apply this in a one-on-one or small group setting.

Journey of Self-Reflection

Bringing everything full circle now, presenting this information in a systematic way takes the learners on a journey through self-reflection. From that self-reflection, the learner is empowered to mold their definition of success and create a future full of endless possibilities. When your learners begin to process this information at a younger age, it will help to maintain the flexibility of their minds. With greater flexibility of mind, students are greater prepared to face the challenges of life. Through this process, we can help education evolve. However, you do not need to just take my word for it. Please read the words, which come directly from a former student, in Figure 1.1.

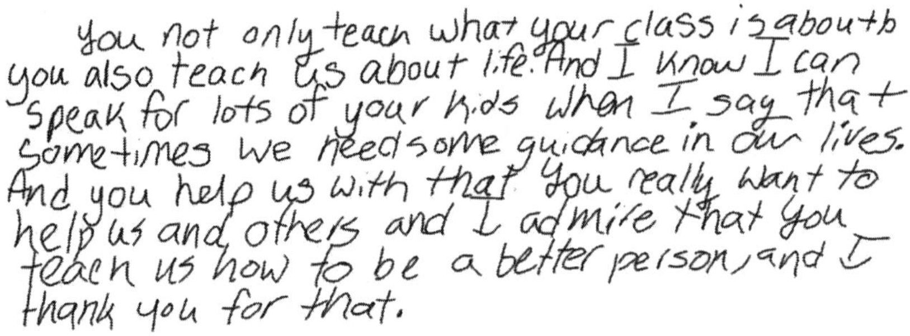

You not only teach what your class is about b you also teach us about life. And I know I can speak for lots of your kids when I say that sometimes we need some guidance in our lives. And you help us with that. You really want to help us and others and I admire that you teach us how to be a better person, and I thank you for that.

FIGURE 1.1 This student quote captures the importance of teaching life lessons.

This student's comments and the other student quotes in these pages came to me unsolicited. At the end of the school year, the language arts department at my school has all the students write letters to adults at the school who have impacted them. The quotes I share come from those letters. But even a thousand quotes will not persuade you to move forward. You must change your mindset and decide how much impact the ideas in this book will have on you and your learners. In a book all about asking the right questions, it begins with you asking yourself a very important one: Are you willing to deeply impact your learners' lives while redirecting your own through the process? If the answer to that is "yes," then there is no limit to how much you can learn as you impact your learners. Now, let's take a look behind the curtain and get a sneak peek of what lies ahead.

Chapter 2: My Personal Struggle in Finding Success

In this chapter, I provide transparency about my failures in life as well as my successes in my education, career, and personal life—elements that helped sculpt me into the person I am today. Those things are the catalyst for the creation of this book.

Chapter 3: Helping Students Find Their Passions: Rapid-Fire Questions and Introducing Bowl Meetings

This chapter introduces quick-reflection questions, which are designed to foster students' understanding of who they are and what they enjoy. Since they have to be dissected by the learner, it helps develop personal understanding as the learners outline a path to their future. It includes having learners reflect on their passion and how they can turn that into a career.

Chapter 4: Evaluating Passion: Shedding Light on Students' Roads to Success

While someone's passion does not automatically lead to a career, understanding how it could is imperative to truly feeling successful. In this chapter, we explore the formula introduced in Chapter 3: Tangible + Purpose = Passion. Also, readers will gleam four tips to help them uncover their passion.

Chapter 5: Victim vs. Value: Leading Students Through Challenging Times and Challenging Labels

The thought-provoking questions contained in this chapter address deeper concepts for students, such as labels, worry, and fear. In addition, it suggests activities teachers (or parents) can use to help students address any negative, self-inflicted mantras they may unconsciously be following.

Chapter 6: Defining Success: Guiding Students to Their Authentic Definition

Everything to this point has led to helping students being able to create an authentic and unique definition of success. This chapter will help them create a "Facets of Success" chart, which enables them to visually chart their progress toward achieving their definition of success. In addition, this chapter introduces the four key components of success.

Chapter 7: Four-Legged Foundation: The Main Components Students Need to Ensure Success

No one can achieve success without understanding the concepts of value, sacrifice, self-discipline, and motivation. This chapter encourages teachers to have a thorough discussion of each topic, centered around a unique engineering design challenge. It includes some tried-and-true examples of how to boost motivation.

Chapter 8: Drain or Gain: Determining What Is Impacting Students' Emotional Health

One of the most important and commonly neglected facets of success is one's emotional state. This chapter lists five areas of life for students to reflect on and evaluate: are these areas draining them or helping to boost them emotionally? This exercise can help teachers evaluate their own lives as well.

Chapter 9: Attainable Goals: Handing Students the Tools for Setting Realistic Dreams

People do not fall into success; they plan for it and work hard to achieve it. This is why it is so crucial to put all the discussions and reflections into action. This chapter walks teachers and learners through what it takes to create specific goals, known by the popular acronym, SMARTER. Additionally, the educators are challenged with some questions of their own to apply to creating a successful classroom.

Chapter 10: Directional Influences—Part I: Who Is Sculpting the Minds of Our Students?

For educators to impact their students more deeply, they need to peel back the layers of "attitude influencers" in students' lives. Three crucial influences—teachers, parents, and social networks—play a pivotal role in students' development and level of success. The better an educator understands the interconnection of all three, the more likely they can guide a student to define success.

Chapter 11: Directional Influences—Part II: Helping Students Tackle Social Media and Their Inner Voice

This chapter concludes the discussion of directional influences with a look at the connections between teacher/parent, student/social, and student/student. Among the issues, we examine how teachers can help students adjust their mindset in order to not allow the negative atmosphere inherent in social media destroy their morale. Also, we take a closer look at changing learners' inner voice, so they don't allow negative thoughts to bring them down.

Chapter 12: Overcoming Defeat: Teaching Your Students to Fail Their Way to Success

Sometimes people must tear down their dreams, goals, and aspirations so they can grow larger than ever imagined. Failure is a necessity and a stepping stone toward learning and triumph. This chapter outlines how students can modify their viewpoints of failure and fail their way to success.

Chapter 13: "Average" Is a Curse Word: Pushing Students to Purge this Toxic Mindset

Regulating fear and recognizing the benefits of failure falls within the student/student attitude influence, meaning both can be regulated within the student mindset. There is another outlook that too often plagues students—maintaining the mindset of "average." Through in-depth reflection, students can purge the tyranny of low expectations. They just need a little nudge from their fearless, above-average educator.

Chapter 14: Lasting Attitude: Addressing that Pesky Negative Mindset with Your Students

After recognizing the flaws in people's attitudes, this chapter discusses what to do to overcome a negative outlook and combat "synthetic" emotions. Most of us are guilty of creating unrealistic, negative emotions in our minds. Here, we discuss how to flip the switch and create more positive emotions. In addition, there are tips that students and adults alike can use to drastically improve their attitudes.

Chapter 15: Pulse on Progress: Checking to See How They Have Improved and a Nice Dose of Credit

No book about creating successful students is complete without addressing some component of finances. One area that today's students—flooded with credit card offers while still in high school—desperately need to be educated about is credit scores. This chapter shows how to convey a wealth of information in just one class lesson. This lesson on credit is a rare gem often not shared.

Chapter 16: Executing the Plan: Realistically Putting All This in Motion

This chapter provides the final push for educators to implement these lessons in their classrooms and with their learners, including an abbreviated outline for classroom adoption. Finally, this is the call to action for teachers to take their students on this reflective journey in order to empower students to take control of their futures. Reflection will help students unravel the past, while action and execution propel them to unlock the future.

References

1. Tyler Schmall, SWNS, "Most Americans Believe School Should Be More Practical," *New York Post*, January 18, 2019, https://nypost.com/2019/01/18/most-americans-believe-school-should-be-more-practical/

2. Geoffrey Chaucer, "The Canterbury Tales: General Prologue," *Poetry Foundation.org*, https://www.poetryfoundation.org/poems/43926/the-canterbury-tales-general-prologue, accessed August 9, 2021.

3. Lory Hough, "What's Worth Learning in School?", *Harvard Ed. Magazine*, Winter 2015, https://www.gse.harvard.edu/news/ed/15/01/whats-worth-learning-school

4. "Start Small, Think Big, Scale Quickly," *The Tony Robbins Podcast*, March 9, 2020, https://www.stitcher.com/show/the-tony-robbins-podcast/episode/start-small-think-big-scale-quickly-spanx-founder-sara-blakely-on-how-to-bootstrap-a-billion-dollar-business-67894720

2

My Personal Struggle in Finding Success

Any time I have enrolled in a training class as an adult, it has been extremely important for me to know the speaker's credentials. For my brain to open up and absorb someone's message, they must have the education or life experience to back that up. So, I want to offer some of my teaching and life credentials.

I have been a full-time public-school teacher since 2003, including a stint at a Title I school, where more than 40% of the students came from a low-income background. I have taught every elementary and middle-grade level, from kindergarten through eighth grade. In elementary schools, I spent seven years as a fifth-grade teacher and two years as a math and science lab teacher. Then I switched to middle school, where I have taught life science, math, physical science, environmental science, STEM subjects (science, technology, engineering, and math), and magic.

I have also worked as an adjunct professor at a nearby college in the evenings and facilitated numerous training courses for educators via working as a Project Lead the Way master teacher. I have won multiple awards for teaching, including Teacher of the Year (twice) and the Air Force Association Teacher of the Year. In addition, I was a National Board-Certified teacher (I let it expire), with a master's degree in math and science education.

DOI: 10.4324/9781003374497-2

Before reviewing my "life" credentials and taking a step further down the path of my own self-reflection, I want to reiterate a statement I shared in Chapter 1: *There is no way to have authentic, life-changing, long-lasting self-improvement without first enduring a soul-searching, gut-wrenching self-reflection.* If you glean nothing else from this book, you and your learners need to internalize that information, since it will give you the framework to understand why I dissect my life in the following paragraphs.

This narrative is going to start in almost reverse order. I wish to describe to you how I think now. Then, I wish to take you back through the events that got me here. At this point in time, I am the strongest emotionally I have ever been. Every day, I wake up happy and full of joy. Let me be clear about something. This is not because the circumstances of my life are so great. Rather, it is because of the mindset I have achieved through putting into practice all that I share in this book.

First, a quick recap of 2019–2020 can help you see that I had plenty of things that could have crushed my spirit.

Pain, Surgery, and a Lobotomy

I sustained a serious injury in January of 2019, which changed my life. It happened on a fun skiing trip with friends to Lake Tahoe, Nevada. Near the end of the second day, I finished one of the most difficult runs I had ever skied. I ended with a successful run through the "Black Diamond" portion, which signifies the steepest, narrowest, and riskiest path on a ski slope. Then, all I had to do was get to the base and grab the lift up again for another run. What I didn't realize was, while I was up on the mountain, the base had warmed up to fifty degrees. For skiers, this was bad news because it meant slushy snow; skis just do not behave the same when maneuvering through slush.

When I reached the base of the mountain, I made a hard left, being sure to keep enough speed to glide right into the queue so I could go back up the lift. The moment I turned left in that slush, my control went haywire, and I collapsed on my left side. When I did that, my left arm flew up. That's when I felt a jarring "pop!"

If you have never endured a traumatic injury, it gives you a feeling that is difficult to describe but includes the realization that *this is no joke*. I somehow climbed to my feet and did my best to ski to the lodge, and then make it back to our hotel.

Fast forward a week. My MRI results had shown I had a torn pectoral tendon. This is what holds your pectoralis muscle (chest) to your humerus (upper arm). Trust me, there was nothing "humerus" about it. When they scheduled me for surgery, I found myself in the midst of a battle in my mind.

Up to this point, beach volleyball was a major component of my life. I would play during the week and a lot on the weekends. Since other players formed my primary social network, the sport represented a significant time commitment. Suddenly, faced with an injury that would keep me sidelined for five months, I had plenty of time to reflect and work on me. Through that process came the writing of this book, as well as some reflection that allowed wounds from both my childhood and adult life to heal. Because of the process I outline in this book of defining success and creating facets of success, I was then prepared for the onslaught of what life would throw at me.

The easiest way to share what happened during 2019 and the first few months of 2020 is to just list them in chronological order. This by no means lessens the impact of these events.

1. January 2019: Shoulder injury, which led to surgery.
2. October 2019: Girlfriend of nearly four years and I part ways.
3. November 2019: Significant neck issues occur, leaving me with three bulging discs and two herniated discs.
4. December 2019: My mother suddenly dies of a heart attack.
5. March 2020: My car's engine cracks just two days before a statewide lockdown because of COVID-19.
6. March 2020: The worldwide pandemic spreads and turns school classes into virtual learning sessions.

I can say with 100% assurance that if I had not gone through the lessons I share in this book and had not been teaching them through these moments, there is no way I could have handled all these challenges. As you can tell, my emotional, physical, and financial health took drastic hits. Part of this journey allowed me to have candid conversations with my mother before she died. This allowed me to have so much more peace of mind than I had ever had before.

Growing Up with Challenges

That catches you up on the 2019–2020 time frame. However, there is much more to my life credentials than just that one-year time span. When I was growing up, my immediate family consisted of Dad, Mom, older sisters Amy and Grace, and me. In 1986, four of the five of us were diagnosed with mononucleosis. At the time, we lived in Rosedale, a small town in southwestern Virginia. Things were pretty rough with Dad being the only one healthy.

Each of us had different symptoms. Mine reared its ugly head with agony centered around my spleen. I have never been stabbed, but I was certain the pain I was enduring was similar. We knew we needed to do something drastic. So, except for Dad, we packed up and drove to Key Largo, Florida to stay in my great-aunt's trailer. (Mom always believed in the healing power of the salt air.) Dad stayed in Virginia to continue his work as a preacher.

Key Largo was a great place to grow up. Having the Atlantic Ocean on one side of me and the Gulf of Mexico on the other made for some great pastimes. Dad eventually joined us, but preaching jobs were few and far between in the Florida Keys. He didn't let that stop him. He marched across US1, the main route through Key Largo, and got hired to help build a new Kmart that was getting ready to open. After it did, Kmart hired him to work there. With five mouths to feed, Dad picked up another job at a local hotel, working in security on the night shift. He has worked two jobs since 1989; at one point that meant 80 hours a week. To outline what his average day looked like back then:

1. Begin first job at 8:30 a.m.
2. Work until 4:00 p.m.

3. Come home, eat, shower, and sleep.
4. Wake up at 9:30 p.m. to make it to job two by 10:30 pm.
5. Work job two until 7:00 a.m.
6. Wash. Rinse. Repeat.

Newton's Laws of Motion are just as applicable to human behavior: For every action, there is an equal and opposite reaction. Thus:

Action = Dad working 80 hours a week
Reaction = Eric must succeed to not have to do that.

My father is obviously a hardworking man, and a highly educated one. He has a master's degree and was even recruited out of high school by NASA because his science scores were so high. (I didn't find out about that until later in life.) I have the utmost respect for him. He did what he thought he had to do to keep food on the table and a roof over our heads. He sacrificed a lot to do what he has done for decades.

However, I didn't want my life to end up that way. Many of the personal reflections I share in this book did not occur until later in life. I firmly believe I could have enjoyed life more if I had had a firm understanding of this topic years ago. This is why I am so driven to write this book and share these topics with as many students and people as I can. Dad working so hard for so many years is a huge motivating factor for me to this day. There were other milestones in my life that forged who I am.

Lack of Sound Advice

Getting educated in Key Largo was interesting. As I mentioned in the preface, small-town life required most of the high school teachers to double up and teach multiple classes, which was why I had the same math teacher three of my four years. This was the same teacher who bolstered my spirits when she took me aside to tell me I had achieved the highest-ever average in her trigonometry class. As fantastic as that was, as I look back, I know what would have been much more impactful: if she would have gone out on a limb and said, "Hey Eric, ever consider a career in math? Here are some great directions and careers you could venture into."

Please don't get me wrong; she was a great teacher. But at that time, I could have used some input from someone in her position to help me sort out my path, or at least get me thinking about my passion. You see, with just a little extra guidance, I could have redirected a decision that became a "major" regret in my life (pun intended).

My whole life I excelled at science and math. But during my senior year of high school, I took a TV production class and won some awards. Without adequate reflection, I decided this should be my college major and career. Four years later, I had a degree in radio/television broadcasting and zipped up to Ohio to work my first full-time job as a news reporter. "Miserable" does not quite encapsulate how I felt in this position, when I was only as good as my last story. When freezing weather struck, I bundled up and trudged out in it. I quickly learned it was not for me.

If only I had evaluated my passions and interests at an earlier age, then I could have seen they revolved around math and science. Had I seen the intersection of my passions, interests, and gifts, this would have been a much more productive path to follow. Plus, I would have had more options for a career. Thus began a festering regret in my life.

After completing my two-year contract, I quit and drove back to Orlando, Florida, where I felt as emotionally lost as I have ever been. I bounced from friend to friend, crashing on a couch or spare bed. Among other things, I worked as a custodian at a church and school, and at one point even worked for a landscaping company—what a filthy job!

All the while, I kept muttering to myself, "Just a few months ago I was on TV five nights a week." I always followed these musings by trying to sort out how on earth I had sunk to such a low place. I was a mess mentally. One of the worst things that would occur during that time would be meeting someone new, when one of the first questions they would ask would be, "Well, what do you do?" I dreaded that question. My identity and definition of success were tied closely to having a title. Not a healthy place to be.

Settling Down

Things began to settle down when a friend of mine, named Brant, let me stay with him indefinitely until I got on my feet. He was a fifth-grade teacher at that time, and I noticed how much he enjoyed his job. I envied that. Thus, I began substitute teaching while continuing to flood news stations with my resume tape.

There was one particular elementary school in Orlando where I spent a lot of time. The other teachers seemed to love me and even rallied to get me hired in a full-time position. Just as that school year was ending, with me working as a substitute teacher, a local news station offered me a position. Ironically, this coincided with an offer of a fifth-grade teaching position from the principal at a school. I snatched up the teaching offer and never contemplated working in TV again.

But that didn't mean the regret was gone. Even deep into my teaching career, I would lament over the "dumb" decisions I had made—specifically, my degree choice of broadcasting. This prompted me to keep learning, and learning, and learning and … *enough already*. Don't get me wrong; the moment we stop learning, we start dying. We should all be (especially educators) lifelong learners. Never stop learning. But, for the sake of your own sanity, make sure what you are learning aligns with your passions, motivations, and definition of success! This was the mistake I made. I hadn't taken a personal inventory to really understand myself.

So, for twenty years, I spent countless hours being cursed to be driven but not knowing my destination. I was dejected. Wallowing around in the regrets of my past, I couldn't appreciate anything my present brought me. In my brain, I had some undefined level of success that I had to obtain, and the only way to get there was to keep moving forward. But what did that mean? I didn't know. For me, the only way I understood to move forward was to just keep learning. So, I did. Even after obtaining my master's degree, I kept taking class after class after class because—in my mind—the wheels had to keep turning. I had to keep moving forward to achieve the goal I thought would provide me happiness.

"When I grow up, I want to be an astronaut."

My early childhood passions for math and science blossomed as a teacher. Still, since I felt so driven, I kept searching for more and more ways that I thought would provide what was lacking in my life. Somehow, I got the idea the best way to have the ultimate impact with math and science would be to become an astronaut. I did a little research and found that with a bit of work on my end, I could match up my resume with the two most recent educator astronauts that NASA had selected.

Since I deeply wanted to be able to positively impact people (students in particular), I felt that being an astronaut would give me a grander platform to affect more lives. Plus, going into space would be amazing! This led me to doing all kinds of learning to put me in a position to be a qualified astronaut candidate. Since most astronauts are engineers, this prompted me to take many engineering courses, even after earning my master's in education. Plus, I got my pilot's certificate and got certified in scuba diving, just to increase my chances.

Seeking Fulfillment

Once again, I had lots of "success" but no fulfillment. A few years ago, I received oodles of awards for being a great teacher. It was very humbling being honored in such a way. I should have been bursting at the seams with joy and happiness. Yet, I still wasn't happy. At those points, I had not defined what success meant to me. I was working on some arbitrary definition. *It was not until I deeply and sincerely understood the content of this book that I began to really appreciate what I had accomplished and had a clear-cut path for my future.* Once I understood these things, my aimless driving came to an end. Once I started sharing these things, I completely understood the path that lay before me.

Far too often, I had been looking at the past, and not focused on the now. A Harvard University study I found confirms I am not alone in my thinking. This study determined nearly 47% of the time people are not focused on the now, meaning they are thinking about the past, or the future, but not the present [1]. Let that settle in on you. Forty-seven percent of the time people don't think about the now. So, for nearly half their life they are thinking about other things. Which means if you are sitting there highly anticipating that vacation coming up in two months, you have a 50/50 chance you will not even be thinking about it when it arrives. Of course, you can be in the "now" and be thinking about the future. More importantly, planning for the future.

Therefore, it is so important that learners begin processing these things now. It is my deep-seated desire that my students and yours not suffer through the wandering process like I followed. It is not enough to ask, "What do you want to be when you grow up?" As educators, it is our duty to set learners on the best road to success by thinking beyond the confines of our subject area. You can have all the education in the world, but if you don't know how to apply it or have a passion for that which you are applying it, then what's the point? My definition of success was severely off balance. I was thinking if I wasn't an astronaut, then I wasn't successful. What a bunch of nonsense.

But enough about me. Let's get to the juicy stuff.

Reference

1. Steve Bradt, "Wandering Mind Not a Happy Mind," *The Harvard Gazette*, November 11, 2010, https://news.harvard.edu/gazette/story/2010/11/wandering-mind-not-a-happy-mind/

3

Helping Students Find Their Passions

Rapid-Fire Questions and Introducing Bowl Meetings

At the beginning of every school year, the first week winds up being a little chaotic. New students, numerous schedule changes and even new admin add to the confusion. This is the optimal time to get to know your students and map out the eye-opening reflective journey they are getting ready to embark upon. Since this entire book is about self-reflection, it would be pointless to just call this chapter and those that follow the "self-reflection" section. That is why the proceeding questions can be administered in a quick more rapid-fire way as opposed to some of the future questions. These questions are especially useful during that first week of school when it is a bit chaotic and when you need to get to know the students.

I really encourage you not to brush past this section. Let me warn you: at first glance, you may dismiss some of them because of their rudimentary appearance. However, it is because of their rudimentary appearance that they are so

DOI: 10.4324/9781003374497-3

effective. That is why I must ask you to trust this process. The questions need to be dissected by the learner. The better the learners grasp their personal understanding, the easier it will be for them to outline a path to their future. Essentially, they need to know who they are before they can ever learn what they want out of life.

There is a bit of embarrassment on my part to admit this, but this portion of the book always makes me think of a movie called *Runaway Bride*. Despite multiple engagements and planned weddings, the main character, played by Julia Roberts, always leaves men standing at the altar. It gets to a point where the male lead, played by Richard Gere, points out she doesn't even know how she likes her eggs cooked because with each previous fiancée she boasted a different choice of preparation. She is challenged to take the time and try eggs prepared in numerous ways in order to sort out her favorite kind. The correlation here is sometimes it takes someone pointing out the questions we need to ask ourselves before we can truly get to know who we are, even if they are seemingly easy questions.

These questions encourage the learner to begin to evaluate themselves from multiple viewpoints, including the viewpoint of their friends and families. In essence, they are laying the foundation to enable them to build their authentic definition of success. Humor me for just a moment and answer this question about yourself. What are you good at doing but don't enjoy? The answer to this question alone can tell you a lot about yourself. Perhaps you are really good at doing trim work and painting at your house, but you absolutely abhor doing it. Now you can cross being a professional painter off your list of career paths! This is why these are not throwaway questions. They force the learner to begin to take a true evaluation of who they are. For reference, here is a rapid glance at the rapid-fire questions. Then we will dive into them a bit more.

Let's take a closer look at some of them now.

1. What are you really good at doing?
2. What is something you enjoy?
3. What is something your friends and family say you are good at doing?
4. Observing what you are good at and what you enjoy, is there any way to use those things in the service of others?
5. In your eyes, what is wrong with the world?
6. What are you bad at doing but wish you were better? What are you bad at doing and *know* you need to be better at? What do your family and friends say you are bad at doing?
7. What are you dying to get better at or learn?
8. What is something that comes very easy to you?
9. What is something you could teach someone else … really well?
10. What is something you could talk about for three hours straight?
11. What skills do you possess that others don't?
12. What makes you feel proud you accomplished?

1. **What are you really good at doing?**
   This requires some deeper explanation to the target audience. The knee-jerk reaction is to rattle off a list of talents. While those are extremely valuable to this question, it is more the overlooked skills that need to be siphoned out by this question that is so vital. Skills and abilities like the following are often overlooked: making friends, problem-solving, talking to new people, public speaking, brainstorming, listening, comforting others, helping others, working alone, or working with others. This list could go on and on. This is why your learners need to look past their lists of obvious talents and look deeper at themselves to adequately answer this question. Notice how they are beginning to develop a list of their marketable skills. I will review this topic further when we discuss adding value.

2. **What is something you enjoy?**
   With this question it is important to make the distinction that they might be good at something, but not enjoy it. The example I give my students is: I am good at cleaning my house, but it is not necessarily something that I enjoy. In addition, when the learner analyzes what they

are good at and what they enjoy, they will obtain further insights. I steer my learners to think how just because you enjoy something, it doesn't mean you are good at it.

As a child, I loved to draw. I would draw Spider-Man and Star Wars characters all the time. But let me tell you, I was not gifted at it... at all! For some reason, I would draw them with a neck and no shoulders. Their arms appeared to grow out of nowhere like a branch. Now, it is okay that I am not good at art. Since I enjoyed it, it served its purpose of lifting my spirits. I knew early on that I was not going to be a professional artist. For any young person seeking to determine a future direction, this is a fantastic realization. Since this process is a reflective one, learning what we are *not good at* serves a purpose. Often, students and learners need to come to this same realization about themselves, especially when it comes to talent-based or sports-based endeavors. There is no shame in admitting you enjoy something, but are not gifted at it. It takes someone with a growth mindset to embrace such knowledge.

3. **What is something your friends and family say you are good at doing?**
   Asking someone else close to you about this can be eye-opening. It gives you a snapshot of how they view you. It can also be a learning experience to see if their answers align with your perceptions.

   Looking at the answers to the first three questions, are there any overlaps? The reflective process will constantly search for them. Finding the overlaps can help learners to piece together their passions. Those passions do not have to become a career, but they could be potential road signs to career choices or just areas that are worth further observation over time. Passions can manifest in a lot of ways in someone's life. In my case, I have been a professional magician for nearly two decades. I started learning magic as an eleven-year-old. While it has never been something I wanted to turn into a full-time career, it is a key part of my life, and one of the facets of my success.

The goal here is to get a learner to consider multiple aspects of their life. By identifying these areas, they can then formulate their ideal definition of success. I will discuss this topic much more later.

4. **Observing what you are good at and what you enjoy, is there any way to use those things in the service of others?**
   This question begins to guide the learner to think more outwardly. When discussing this question, I remind students to think in terms of what someone would be willing to pay you to do *and* in terms of how you can help others. My emphasis is never to solely get them to think in terms of a paycheck, but also from a larger global impact.

5. **In your eyes, what is wrong with the world?**
   The answers to this question can reveal what the learners notice about the world. It can also spotlight an area that concerns them. This could be a topic they wish to pursue and work to improve in the world. This can even start to point them to an overriding life purpose.

6. **What are you bad at doing but wish you were better? What are you bad at doing and *know* you need to be better at? What do your family and friends say you are bad at doing?**
   I combine these questions because they are meant for learners to dive into. I want them to examine areas of their lives where they could use improvement. I tell my students I don't pose these questions to destroy their self-esteem. I simply ask them because for them to make true gains in life, they must identify weaknesses or areas where they need to improve. The first two questions seem similar, but the words "wish" and "know" drastically alter them. To the first, most students respond with a discussion of their talents. With the second, I was shocked by the transparency students displayed regarding areas in which they know they need to improve. Students have shared things like wanting to complete tasks they start, to be more focused, and to become more outgoing to meet more people.

Prior to asking these questions, I prepare the learners by discussing how performers and athletes video themselves while they are performing or playing. Then they analyze the video to make improvements. I am embarrassed to say the first time I saw myself performing a magic show, I was appalled to watch myself walk all around the performance area like the Energizer Bunny. I wouldn't stop moving! It would have made the audience motion sick. However, through that video I learned how to enhance my performance. The recording allowed me to see "bad" things I could correct. Without it, I would have never improved. This is why learners need to dive into the not-so-pretty sides of their thinking and behaviors. The waters might be cold and murky, but they are extremely cleansing and eye-opening.

That brings me to the last set of questions:

A. What are you dying to get better at or learn?
B. What is something that comes very easy to you?
C. What is something you could teach someone else … really well?
D. What is something you could talk about for three hours straight?
E. What skills do you possess that others don't?
F. What makes you feel proud you accomplished?

Each of the six above questions do not need further discussion. I lumped them together because they are all meant to challenge the learners to understand themselves more deeply. You do not need to spew them at learners all at once; let them digest them a couple at a time.

Implementation Process

I review the previous rapid-fire reflection questions over a series of days, spending just a few minutes of class time discussing the goal of each of the questions. Then, the students answer them, writing the answers in the back of their notebooks and working forward. This way they have a running document of their answers. It is also enjoyable to have the learners revisit their answers months later to see if they still agree with their "younger" selves.

For the questions that follow, though, I spend more class time discussing them. They require some more in-depth thought. To implement these questions, I use something called a "Bowl Meeting."

What Is a Bowl Meeting?

A Bowl Meeting is the tool I use to deliver my message to my students. It is an easy way for you to disseminate this information among your learners when you are working with a class or a small group. The ease of implementing the Bowl Meeting is what allows you to reach so many learners and discover more about them at the same time. In Figure 3.1, the student quoted has summed up Bowl Meetings quite well. They are that simple. Prior to students entering my classroom, I set out printer paper (precut into eighths) for students. I instruct them to grab a piece of paper on their way in and answer the question prompt on the board.

> Also, he teaches us things that we never would learn in school at any other points in our education. He gives us a prompt, we write a response on a small slip of paper, and then we put the papers into a bowl. We spend the entire class period discussing the topic, and the students' responses. I really like how these days give us a break from the usual things we do every day.

FIGURE 3.1 This student articulates the definition of "Bowl Meetings" well.

Once completed, they bring the piece of paper up and place it into a bowl. They then pull their chairs around and sit in a designated area. Thus begins our Bowl Meeting, where everyone's answer is shared. Essentially, I am having a class meeting. Later, I will discuss the benefits of classroom meetings in more detail, but for now I just want to emphasize the power of these meetings and encourage you not to dismiss this idea because of its simplicity.

Bowl Meeting Question: What Are You Passionate About and How Can You Turn That into a Career?

That really is the million-dollar question that many adults cannot even answer. Oddly enough, children can often answer that question more easily than adults. I have speculated a lot about why that is. First, children are still in the mindset of learning. Therefore, they have a growth mindset and an openness to explore their options for the future. Second, life sneaks up on us rather quickly. Individuals start following a path and before they know it, five or even ten years have slipped away. By that time, their dreams have faded, along with their motivation to pursue them.

However, the primary reason children can answer it is because they are asked about their futures with regularity. Think about it. When was the last time someone asked you what you are passionate about? Life settles in and legitimate excuses take the place of legitimate dreams. Dreams without action are just dreams. Unfortunately—more often than not—adulthood is where dreams go to die. This is why it is so important to have learners not just discuss what they want to do when they grow up, but map out how to make that a reality.

Before diving any further into the discussion of passion, let's have a quick discussion on the maturation process of passion. At a young age, passion is very tangible. A child might be passionate about art, singing, basketball, or any number of different things. As we age, passion becomes more about the end product. If you slave away at a job every day where you have no investment in the end goal of that job, that is stress. But if you slave away at a job every day and are fully invested in the end goal, that is passion. It is no longer about the day-to-day nuances of the act; it is about the end goal. That end goal could be described as impacting others, helping others, furthering our knowledge, bettering the world, attacking hunger, or other important outcomes.

Let me give you a more tangible example. As I mentioned earlier, at a young age, I enjoyed math and science. Those were very tangible concepts for me. I later discovered I also enjoy being creative and speaking in front of others. Again, these are tangible concepts. Because of all these things, I thoroughly enjoy teaching my subject area of STEM. It is always changing, and my students really enjoy it. However, those tangible things need to be tied to a purpose. For me, that purpose is what I am deeply passionate about: impacting others in a positive way. Teaching is a great platform for me to accomplish that end goal. To explain it as a mathematical formula:

$$Tangible + Purpose = Passion$$

Let's create a working definition of tangible and purpose. Tangible concepts are attributes that a person can easily identify about themselves. For example: athletic, good at math, enjoy people, love to learn in isolation, or enjoy writing. These are just a few of the nearly infinite examples of tangible concepts. These are the things the rapid-fire questions I listed earlier draw out of a learner. A definition of purpose could mean a person wishes to have great impact, help others, heal others, and so many other possibilities.

Learners need to go through the process of first identifying their "tangible" attributes. Then, they can begin to realize their purpose and true passion. The lively discussions that typically follow the question, "What am I passionate about and how can I turn that into a career?" help learners make connections between their current lives and what the future could hold.

Exploring Passion

At the outset, I just gently have them reflect on the question, which works like a formative assessment. Essentially, you get a jumping-off point to knowing what they currently deeply desire to do. You also get to evaluate how much knowledge they have about the topic and how much thought they have given it before prompting them to conduct more in-depth research on their passion. This is when you can discuss the details on a common dream many young people have, of one day becoming a professional athlete. I ask them: is it possible to have a career in this sport that they love so much? Don't get me wrong; I am not telling them NOT to work toward their dream, but consider perhaps careers that can support their passion. For example, a trainer or physical therapist could keep a person involved in the sport they love without needing the exceedingly rare skills possessed by professional athletes.

Is it their passion to become a videogame designer? Do they love art? Great. Then could they use their abilities in 2D art to become a video game designer? Or produce graphic designs in demand by any number of commercial enterprises that will support them financially while they pursue their dream of painting portraits on the weekends? I do not squash their dreams, but try to frame them in a way that they can see multiple options that connect to the field they love.

It is vital to not blow a bunch of hot air at students or other group of learners and feed them some empty line like: "You can be whatever you want to be." That is not true. Let me explain. Take that passion they just dreamed about and have them ask themselves if it is also a gift. Do they have the tangible skillset required? Think of it this way: they might be passionate about music, but severely lack the "gift" required to be a great musician. Perhaps they are truly passionate about football, but if they stand five-foot-two, can't lift the bag out of the trash can, or run the 40-yard dash in two minutes, they aren't likely to make the NFL. See the difference?

To plot out the tremendous amount of potential a learner possesses, they have to be honest with themselves and decide what they are passionate about and gifted at when it comes to making a career choice more than a wish. Think about all these amateur talent shows. No doubt, you have heard someone perform and said to yourself, "Who told them they could sing?" That contestant might have a passion, but not a gift or the tangible assets required to succeed in that area. No one person can be great at everything. There is nothing wrong with someone admitting that they are not gifted at something, or that they do not have the tangible skills for something. This is part of the learning process. Remember, true growth only comes on the other side of self-reflection.

In a conversation I had with a close person in my life around the topic of passion and her job, she enlightened me on this subject. When I asked her if her job is her passion, she said she would not consider her job her passion, but it allows her to combine many of the things she is passionate about under one roof— she loves data analysis and problem-solving. It was eye-opening for me to apply her response in thinking about the connection to learners. Your job doesn't have to be your passion. It should, however, contain many of the things you are passionate about. This prompts the need for self-reflection even more. The more a learner can dissect their personal passions, the more likely they can find a job that is fulfilling.

Mapping It Out

A person should track and map their passions as early as possible. The tracking takes very little time since most learners can answer the "passion" portion of the question easily. If they can't, do not worry; I will review more on this topic later. It is the mapping portion that is vitally important and requires a bit more time. Allow your students or learners to research what requirements are necessary for a career in their passion of choice.

Here is a list of questions you can assign to them. If you are an educator, this could make a great homework assignment. You will notice how similar these questions are to the ones in the introductory, rapid-fire section. There is no harm in asking the same question more than once. At times, learners' answers will change.

1. What do you enjoy doing?
2. What are you good at doing?
3. What do others say you are good at doing?
4. Are there any careers that combine these tangible things?
5. Do any of those careers interest you?
6. Pick one of those careers.
7. What education (formal or not) do you need to have to obtain this career?
8. Where can you get this education?
9. If it is not provided in the formal setting, then how will you obtain this knowledge?
10. How much money will it cost to achieve this knowledge?
11. How much time will it cost?
12. How in demand is this career?
13. How much money can you make on the high and low ends of this career?
14. Who is someone you can research who has succeeded in this career?
15. What other specific skills will you need to have to make it in this field? (Meaning soft skills like communication, teamwork, problem-solving, and work ethic.).
16. What is the likelihood you can obtain this as a career?

Each of these questions is essential to them mapping out a potential career following their passions. No matter how obscure, silly, or statistically unlikely their passion might be, let them do the research. This will set the stage for them to truly begin to understand the task that lies ahead. Plus, it will give them the opportunity to begin setting their specific goals for obtaining this career.

At this point, I challenge them to go home and write down today's date and what they said they are passionate about. I tell them to write it some place permanent like inside their closet. Then, in four months, reevaluate, and write down what their passion is at that moment on the wall. Then again, and again. Every four months write it down. Then, when it comes to what path they should follow, they have a perfect history of their passion. If their passion stays consistent, then they are truly on to something. But by no means keep it hidden there. Encourage them to tell people about their passion. Share it with everyone.

Shout it from the rooftops! This will allow educators and others know how to support them.

A great example of how an educator can support a student's passion is described by *New York Times* best-selling author Brad Meltzer. In one of his books, he tells the story of his high school writing teacher. When she met him, she wasted no time identifying his future potential. She recognized that he was a great writer and really had no place being in her classroom. She quickly jumped into action and told him to just ignore what she was talking about in class, and just write. He did. Now, he has sold millions of books because his teacher went above and beyond for him and fanned the flames of his passion. In this circumstance, his teacher decided her content was secondary. She recognized putting him on a path to success was her main goal [1].

Now to the example I mentioned in the preface, about the student with exceptional artistic talent. Judging by her reaction to my suggestion that I pay her to draw me a picture, it was as if I had offered her a million dollars. You should have seen her face light up! She would come to class every day and show me the progress she made. Figure 3.2 is her drawing. I leave you to judge its artistic merit.

FIGURE 3.2 My former student's amazing artwork.

Today, it hangs in the room at my house where I store all my magic props. Now, I have an original piece of art and she knows how amazing her talent is and how it can lead to a career. I am doing my best to encourage students like her in their passion.

The exciting thing about this topic of passion and careers is: if you are an educator, it allows you to make a career connection to your subject area. If you haven't already, consider bringing in individuals from the community working in your subject area to talk to your class. This is such an important step (so important, you will notice me mentioning this several times). Teaching STEM lends itself to community involvement quite easily. I have the bomb squad showcase their robots for my robotics class. NASA, Lockheed, and Frito Lay engineers come and present and lead field trips for my groups. A bear biologist even came to my class to enlighten my class about the issue with bears getting into trash cans. This launched an engineering design challenge with my students to build a "bear proof" trash can.

Please consider looking for opportunities in your community that relate to your subject area. Each opportunity you can provide gives your students that much more information about selecting a career. Knowledge can be power if executed correctly. Let's empower our students with as much knowledge as we can. If you are not an educator, but are choosing to share this information with someone important in your life, you still can make real world connections like those mentioned here for your learner.

ⓥ Key Takeaways

1. Using rapid-fire questions with students gets their reflective juices flowing.
2. Bowl Meetings are a great way to set up class meetings.
3. By researching their passion, students can begin to piece together a path for their future.
4. Connecting one's tangible strengths with a purpose can direct a learner to what could be a passionate career.
5. Tangible + Purpose = Passion.

💬 Points to Ponder—Chapter 3

1. Which of these questions do you wish you had understood when you were younger?
2. How do you implement class meetings already in your classroom?
3. How do you like your eggs?

Reference

1. Brad Meltzer, "World's Greatest Teacher," *BradMeltzer.com*, December 2012, https://bradmeltzer.com/TV-Kids-and-More/918/worlds-greatest-teacher

4

Evaluating Passion

Shedding Light on Students' Roads to Success

Passion isn't a simple topic to explore. Invariably in the classroom or at speaking presentations, someone will ask: "What if I don't know what I'm passionate about?" That is a fantastic question, which could take a long time to answer. After all, it took me decades to sort it out. By starting the discussion of that question, though, we can expedite the process. Do those passions always translate to a career? Maybe. That is why it is a process to discover your passions, because passions can change, especially for younger people as they mature. Also, passions can change with additional knowledge and education, which they could attain.

Circling back to what I discussed at the introduction of this topic, it lies in the learner identifying the "tangible" concepts, such as history, math, dancing, and football. Then sorting out the "purpose" concepts, such as impacting others or creating a product that helps people. Remember the formula I introduced in the previous chapter:

$$\text{Tangible} + \text{Purpose} = \text{Passion}$$

There are plenty of questions that can be used to prompt learners to reflect on what potentially their passion could be.

DOI: 10.4324/9781003374497-4

I introduced some in the rapid-fire reflection section. However, if they still struggle getting the juices of their passion fruit flowing, have them contemplate the following:

1. If you had an hour of free time right now, what would you do?
2. If you could talk about anything for the rest of your life, what would it be?
3. What would you spend a thousand dollars on, right now?
4. What is one activity that, if you did it, you are confident you would produce superb results?

An additional question I like to pose is: What energizes you? For many people, they get energy from interacting with others. Some people are energized from pouring themselves into solving a problem. As learners understand these traits about themselves, the path to a career based on their passion can become clearer. Another way to sort out one's passion is to plug responses to the following questions into Figure 4.1.

FIGURE 4.1 Three questions student use to sort out their passion.

You will notice in this example, the questions: (1) What do you excel at? and (2) What do you enjoy doing? both align with what I mentioned as tangible concepts. The question, How do you want to impact the world? connects with purpose. The overlap of these three things is where passion lies.

Encourage your learners to carve out some time to just let their minds wander and for those previous questions to marinate. They can't expect it to become clear in a matter of seconds. They have to let their minds discover what their passion is and where their heart wants to go. Along with these, here are some ideas to help your learners navigate the road. Each one requires learners to spend time reflecting on who they are.

1. **Gut check! Attitude.**

   In order to find their passion in life, students must have the right attitude. They have to go into this journey with the mindset that they will succeed and find what they are looking to accomplish. If "can't" enters into their psyche, then they are right. If they say they can't sort out what they want to do or find out, then they are right. Earl Nightingale was a network broadcaster, life coach, and motivational speaker from the 1950s until his death in 1989. He has a great thought on this topic:

> "Success is the result of a good attitude."
>
> Earl Nightingale [1]

   Guess what your role is as an educator for this first step? You must be the cheerleader and the leader of the pep rally. You must show them the attitude they must have. Rarely in life do opportunities—good or bad—appear when we want them. We must have the right attitude when they arrive. If you have a poor attitude about your job or the subject you teach, then so will they! After all, attitude reflects leadership. Have them reflect on a time when they had a bad attitude and it turned out to be a great opportunity! You can use this as one of your class discussions. Share with them that they can succeed at something and still feel like a failure if their attitude is in the wrong place. Essentially, we are getting them to think about thinking. There will be a much more in-depth look at "attitude" later.

2. **Brain check! Remain teachable.**

> Education leads to learning. Learning leads to passion. Passion leads to options.

Education plays a pivotal role sorting out a person's passion. Remaining teachable does not necessarily mean constantly being immersed in formal education. It means embracing and sustaining a mindset that is always willing to hear new ideas and bounce them against old ones. It means when an interest pops up, a learner follows that interest and learns more about it. If that interest wanes, then that is not the course for the learner. If the interest blossoms and they just can't learn enough on the topic, then they might be on to something. The only way anyone can discover their passion is if they approach each subject with an open mind and the correct attitude. It means establishing and maintaining a growth mindset.

What is your goal as the facilitator of learning for this second step? Lead by example. Always remain teachable yourself. Show them this. Share with your students what you are learning and how you are learning it. Allow your learner or learners to teach you something. In itself, this will make a lasting impression on them.

3. **Smell check! When you catch a whiff, follow the scent; take action.**

    If a learner has the right attitude, remains open-minded and teachable, when they catch a whiff of something they like, they should see where it leads. Basically, take action. That smell might lead to a trash can or an undiscovered flower garden. They have to be ready to follow the path and see if it turns into a real passion or just a phase. Here is an excerpt from a student, Noah, who took my magic class. He was thirteen at the time.

I've learned so much. Magic class, what you taught me wasn't magic, it was social skills. The ability to walk up to anyone, start a conversation and be comfortable doing it. And that's such important skill. And I'm so grateful that you that you taught me, and that I'll never forget. I hope to continue practicing the skills I've learned in your class. This path I'm going down is one I'm proud to say you put me on.

[Noah F.]

As of the writing of these words, Noah is twenty-one years old and a firefighter, but he is getting paid hundreds of dollars an hour to perform magic around town. Talk about following the scent. He is crazy passionate about performing magic. Whether he turns this into a career or not, he sure has a great side hustle. Notice he was open to learning something new, recognized it as a passion, and is following the direction it is leading him. The cool thing is he has inspired me to grow my magic business because his passion is so contagious.

For you as an educator to help in this step, you need to present ways for students to follow their passions. Bring in guest speakers, take them on field trips, and do something so students can see how their passions can equate to a career.

4. **Heart check! Evaluate your skill set**.

This is an ongoing process for *everybody*, but especially students! Learners should never stop assessing their talents and gifts. When reflecting on a career, if they know math is not their strong suit, then charging down a career path with a lot of math might not be the way to go. However, they might have a magnetic personality. Then, the sky's the limit in regard to working in public relations, broadcasting, or sales. They need to truly evaluate what they have to offer. Then, see how those talents are best used in a career.

Now, don't get me wrong: if a student is weak in a subject area, they can overcome that weakness by putting in hard work. Look at Homer Hickam Jr. He has written multiple books, one of which (*Rocket Boys*), was made into a hit movie, *October Sky*. Hickam admitted math was not his strong suit, but he still went on to be a NASA engineer. How? He worked hard and had the heart to prove it.

Once again, for you, this means helping to point out at an early stage a learner's strengths and weaknesses. Don't discourage him or her from pursuing a dream. Help break down the strong points they have that can help them achieve their dream. Also, point out areas of weaknesses they will need to bulk up before going down that path. This links back to those rapid-fire questions they have already answered.

These steps can be the springboard for students to discover their passions. They are not a sure-fire plan, but the more they think, reflect, and observe, the more likely they will be able to truly define their passion and how to turn it into a career.

Wait, Is He Contradicting Himself?

While you might be asking that question about now, remember that connecting passion and a career is a way of getting the learner to analyze a potential path for their career. Passion alone will not and does not always lead to a career. It can be an indicator of something the learner *could* do. Understanding one's personal passion is a significant step in self-awareness and building a true definition of success. Just because there is "passion" for a topic or an area, you should always watch for some cautionary flags waving when following your passion. Passion is very similar to love: it can be blind. Therefore, learners need to recognize on their own that perhaps their passion is irrationally based and will not lead to a career.

I know this sounds contradictory to what I have previously stated. I gently touched on this idea when pointing out a student should examine if their passion is also a gift. There is a thin line between following a passion that can turn into a career and following it blindly, no matter what the consequences. As with people in love, students will need to come to their own realization of the longevity of their passion and likelihood of turning it into a full-time career, or concluding that it will just be a great hobby. Once again, with further education on the topic of their passion, some of that realization can occur. That is why it is so important to allow your learners to research those previously listed questions. I have had students change their minds about their passion becoming a career after they did some additional research.

Gauging the Statistics

By now, you have probably guessed to where I am leading this conversation: sports. We are living in a media-hyped age of widespread athletic visibility, driven by the gargantuan-sized salaries accorded professional athletes. With even high school sports now televised nationally, countless numbers of parents have grown delusional about the prospects of their child becoming the next millionaire (or billionaire). They believe that if they stick a golf club in their child's hands at the age of three, the kid will be the next Tiger Woods—the same for a ball creating the next phenom in football, basketball, or soccer. Don't get me wrong, there are many valuable skills students learn from playing sports—things like collaboration, teamwork, and better communication. But the fact of the matter is: far too many students are sacrificing their bodies at way too early an age as they develop an utterly blind devotion to a sport.

Growing up, I loved playing basketball and love playing beach volleyball to this day, so I know what kind of obsession sports can create. But it pains me to see students who are not introduced to other avenues and activities that have a much higher likelihood of becoming a career, all because of the blind steering of their parents or their own sports cravings.

The challenge emerges when dedication to the sport sacrifices other areas of a student's development and health. The highest chance of a high school athlete advancing to a higher level occurs in men's ice hockey. They have an 11.3% of playing at the collegiate level and a miniscule 0.16% (less than 0.2 of 1%!) of making it professionally. For all the other sports I researched, the chances are even less. [2] It is scary to think how many knees, hips and backs are being sacrificed for a miniscule chance of making it "big."

As part of students' research into their passion, please direct them to look at the chances of actually getting into the field which they are so passionate about. That is one of the questions on that list for them to research. As mentioned before, encourage them to try new things. Who knows where it may lead? The goal, of course, is that it leads them to an enjoyable, success-filled career. Later, I am going to refer back to this section in discussing what value students should bring to the table along with their involvement in sports.

Changing Direction

If the topic of careers in professional sports is discussed in an honest and sincere way, students will take to heart what you are saying and contemplate the likelihoods. Take the example of a former student of mine named Peyton. His straight, floppy hair had the girls swooning and he handled that attention quite well. With a passion for skateboarding, he really fitted the stereotype of what you think someone out skating on the boardwalks in California would look like.

Peyton took my STEM class for three years. During two of those years, he stated he wanted his passion of skateboarding to turn into a professional career. His talent caught the attention of others: by seventh grade he already had sponsors. I never discouraged him from his dream, even going to see him skate once. He was quite good.

The reason I bring him up is because at the start of his eighth-grade year, he stunned me with his statement that he wanted a career in 2-D graphic design. I was shocked! Immediately, I asked what had happened to his skateboarding because I didn't want him to give up on that dream. Peyton replied, "It is still there, but I want something to fall back on." What a tremendous shift in his mindset. This all stemmed from repeated, honest discussions with my class.

With another former student, I flat out encouraged him to chase his dream of a becoming a professional athlete. Cedric possessed a quality about him to be a true leader. Yes, he loved football, but he wanted to use its visibility as a platform to help others. That is why I encouraged him 100% to follow his dream of becoming a professional athlete. It is not sports nor the pursuit of sports I dislike, it is the blind pursuit of them without having a higher goal in mind that troubles me.

Before leaving the topic of passion, I wish to discuss a quote with you from the book *Grit: The Power of Passion and Perseverance*. The author, Angela Duckworth, is a psychology professor at the University of Pennsylvania. Her TED talk on grit has been viewed by more than ten million people. She does a tremendous job digging into the topic of discovering your passion.

> Passion for your work is a little bit of discovery, followed by a lot of development, and then a lifetime of deepening.
> —Angela Duckworth [3]

Angela Duckworth's statement summarizes everything I am trying to convey. Learners must be open-minded to discover their passion. They also have to be willing to invest time to truly develop the idea and concept beyond what I call the "honeymoon stage." In addition, they must be willing to continually learn and hone their craft.

After completing the Bowl Meeting on the topic of passion and turning that into a career, I give each student the list of the sixteen questions that start with: "What do you enjoy doing?", which I listed in Chapter 3 (see page 23. You will also find them as a resource at the end of the book in Appendix D).

I then assign the students to research the answers to these questions, which allows them to begin to digest the potential road that lies ahead of them. I have them tape the small piece of paper where they answered the prompt question, along with the form containing the answer to these research questions, in the back of their notebooks. They will want this information at a later date when they make their "time capsule" (more about that later).

Now, it's on to the next chapter and a question that is as significant as the issue of passion: what attributes do you want your future self to have?

✓ Key Takeaways

1. When students are uncertain of their passion, they can reflect on:
   a. What do you enjoy doing?
   b. How do you want to impact the world?
   c. What do you excel at?
2. Just because a student is passionate about something does not mean they need to pursue it as a career.
3. Students should be aware of blindly following a passion especially when it comes to sports.

♡ Points to Ponder—Chapter 4

1. How are you stacking up being an educator?
2. Does this meet your definition of how you want to impact the world?
3. What challenges will your students face when answering the question of how they want to impact the world?

References

1. Earl Nightingale, *QuoteFancy*, https://quotefancy.com/quote/797 680/Earl-Nightingale-A-great-attitude-is-not-the-result-of-success-success-is-the-result-of-a, accessed August 14, 2021
2. Luke Kerr-Dineen. 2016. ftw.usatoday.com. July 27. https://ftw.usatoday.com/2016/07/here-are-your-odds-of-becoming-a-professional-athlete-theyre-not-good
3. Angela Duckworth, *Grit: The Power of Passion and Perseverance* (New York: Scribner, 2018), 103.

5

Victim vs. Value

Leading Students through Challenging Times and Challenging Labels

The social distancing and remote learning that became watchwords during the COVID-19 pandemic thrust millions of teachers onto a hybrid teaching platform. I was one of them. This meant I was teaching a portion of my students face-to-face while others attended my class virtually. That balancing act is not the best teaching model, but it was born out of necessity.

One of the greatest challenges I faced was student participation. There was no way to "force" students at home to actively engage in class, which at times meant turning on their cameras and microphones. I tried every tactic I know: being nice or mean, rewarding, motivating, ignoring, and a slew of others. You name it, I tried it. My last resort was contacting parents. Once I did that, I identified the explanations why students weren't participating—excuses. I heard the gamut of excuses for non-participation. In essence, they revolved around the "victim mentality."

This experience led to an impromptu discussion with one of my classes about "Victim vs. Value." At the heart of this juxtaposition lies a key question I often ask my students:

DOI: 10.4324/9781003374497-5

Bowl Meeting: What Attributes Do You Want Your Future Self to Have?

The reason I explore this topic is because I believe the education system frequently negatively impacts students by placing labels on them. It starts at an early age. Those labels can range from "gifted" to "ADHD" to "IEP" (which stands for Individualized Education Program) to a slew of others.

From that moment on, the victim mentality begins. Teachers and parents begin to identify that student by their label; parents especially use them as crutches or excuses for their child not performing. The challenge children face is how to overcome those excuses. I am not trying to be insensitive, but the real world—outside of academia—cares not one whit about those labels, only about what a person can produce.

So, if a learner has those labels, they must adapt to overcome them in order to focus on their productivity. I know gifted individuals and former students who have not produced a single thing to better their lives or the society around them. Yet, I know individuals who struggled with ADHD while in school, but today lead amazing lives. What is the difference? The latter received the labels, but decided to not allow that to define them. They chose to not be the victim of a label.

In life, the most devasting labels we receive originate with ourselves. They occur when we look in the mirror. The thoughts that follow can be paralyzing. Young learners frequently need to evaluate what labels they are placing upon themselves. Growing up in a small town, my high school had less than 650 students in all four grades. Because of that, I was limited in my comparisons with other people. But today, learners face continual comparison with every individual in their schools, plus everyone they follow or friend via social media.

In most cases, the first thing students do in the morning is reach for their phones. When that happens, let the comparison begin! The inundation of information and comparison could cause even the most secure person to waver. When you are constantly looking at others who are literally posting a doctored snapshot of their lives or accomplishments, it is difficult not to engage in comparisons. Then, while looking in a mirror, many individuals adopt the victim mentality, repeating such mantras as, "I am not as pretty as her" or "I am not as strong as him." Such thoughts meddle with their minds, leaving them feeling like a victim. In reality, they are not victimized by someone else, but by their own mindset.

Combating Mantras

The challenge I extended to my students was this: Every time those negative mantras rear their ugly heads, combat them with three positive attributes about yourself that you like. We can't always control our first thought, but we can reduce the impact of it by quickly negating it with three others that resonate more emotionally. This then changes them from becoming a victim to adding value to their lives.

The informal nine-minute discussion I had that day preceded an activity I did with my students a week later, allowing them to share their answers with the group. I asked the students to close their eyes and visualize themselves in ten years. We started with their physical attributes; I asked them to imagine such things as whether they were tall, smiling, well-built, overweight, somewhere in between, or had good posture. Next, I asked them about their mental attributes. In essence, if someone were to meet their future self, how would they describe them? Smart? Hard-working? Caring? Kind? I listed off about a dozen adjectives. Then, I asked them to draw the simple chart shown in Figure 5.1 in the back of their notebook.

FIGURE 5.1 This chart helps learners envision their future selves.

I proceeded to ask them to fill in as many adjectives as they could, depicting what they want their future self to be like. After sharing those, I asked them to fill in the left side of the chart with a comparison. If they wrote "smart" on the right, and they were smart now, they would reflect each other. But if they wrote "self-disciplined" on the right, but they weren't now, then they would write something like "lazy" in contrast. The challenge was to get them to define what they wanted to be like in the future, contrasting that with their current attributes.

In addition, I told them they needed to evaluate where they stood now in order to make the desired modifications to become that person in the future. My goal was not to demean them, but to get them to take a true inventory of themselves and challenge them to become the person they wished to be. I concluded the discussion by challenging them to be just a quarter of a percent better today than they were yesterday. And each day be just a quarter of a percent better that day than the day before. It is the small steps that lead to completing a long journey.

In a small side note, during the first discussion of victim vs. value, I had a parent listening in virtually, although I had no idea because the student's camera was turned off. Immediately after the discussion, I received an email from the parent. I am omitting some of it for personal reasons, but want to capture its essence.

> I heard the lecture you just gave in (my daughter's) class today. You are 100 percent correct. I am so glad you talked about that ... And I needed to hear that too.

After a personal story, she concluded:

> But I know that's playing the victim, and I know I have to stop that. So, I really needed to hear that today. Thank you. You are an amazing teacher, an amazing person, and (my son) and (my daughter) are very fortunate to have you as a teacher.

An administrator popped into that same virtual meeting and gave me an evaluation. I had no idea she was going to do that.

It went well; I share that not to brag, but to cite as additional evidence that this message needs to be proclaimed—to everyone.

Flip the Script

A few days after teaching this lesson, I circle back to it with the students (not a full-blown Bowl Meeting, just a few minutes of class). Since I have mentioned to them earlier how important it is to have three positive attributes ready when they begin to recite those negative "mantras" about themselves, I take time to allow them to script out those positive attributes. In such discussions, I am 100% transparent. I bring up how, when I look in the mirror, 90% of the time all I see is my huge Hungarian nose (thanks, Dad.) In an effort to flip the script, I make sure to also be grateful for my full head of hair, green eyes, and slim build. Sharing this with the learners is an effort to get them to be deeply reflective.

This is why I add the follow-up prompt to the negative mantras:

Bowl Meeting: Name Three Attributes You Like about Yourself

One of them must be a physical attribute. I added that last qualifier because students would commonly rattle off things like smart, funny, or athletic. Those are great, but I wanted to make sure to address a physical characteristic, since that can be such a common insecurity for learners.

Another question I pose (sometimes in a Bowl Meeting and other times in a smaller group):

Bowl Meeting: What Do You Worry about the Most?

Because of the personal nature of this topic, it might not be a full-on Bowl Meeting: I don't necessarily have students openly share their responses, just those who wish to do so. If you want to get a snapshot into a learner's mind, ask them what they worry about the most. It will reveal quickly what they care about. Their answers can reveal insecurities, but more often than not they reveal fears (more on fear later).

For the students and learners, this is a good way to ease into the discussion. The reason I use the term "worry" instead of "fear" is because, when asked what they fear, learners (especially younger ones) immediately attach the question to tangible—but often irrational—things like snakes or spiders. Using the word "worry" in the question invites learners to think more emotionally. Thus, they gain a greater understanding of themselves and the way they think. Essentially, it allows them to understand what is most important to them.

To go out on a limb here, I would say that every person has some sort of worry in their life. The level and complexity may vary greatly, as will how much they allow that worry to impact their lives. Just from asking this question in one class, I received answers such as:

◆ "Slowly becoming a burden to everyone I meet."
◆ "Losing all my friends and not being able to make new ones."
◆ "Losing my family because of something I have done."

These are far more reflective and transparent answers than I ever would have imagined receiving from middle schoolers. The depth of these answers is the reason to have this discussion. By no means am I trying to create unneeded worry in the students' lives, but this topic allows the learners to establish what will later be a major facet of their success.

Defining Worry

After allowing the students to share their worries, I ask which of the following categories their worry most would likely fall into: family, friends, money, future, physical health, mental health, or other. These categories wind up being the facets of success they establish later. For now, I use this data to help them understand that they are not alone in their worries.

I then proceed to ask them if they can toggle the word "worry" with fear in the statement, "I worry most about…". Of course, they can. At this point, I am very delicate how I share this with the learners because I do not wish for them to feel as if I am negating their worry. This is when I transition the discussion to FEAR—or False Expectations Appearing Real. Their worries and fears may or may not ever happen. The important thing is to strengthen their minds for the day they perhaps occur. To phrase it another way: preparing their minds for the storms of life.

The large majority of our fears and worries stem from things we cannot control. For the learners, and myself included, this is a fantastic time to remind them we control the things we can and prepare our minds to respond in a healthy way when life tosses at us things we can't control. *This is the key; we can only control our response to the challenging moments in life.* We can't control when or how those worries come to fruition, but we can be prepared for them and then have the appropriate response.

In order to have an appropriate, healthy response to storms, people must work on balance in their lives. How can they have balance without understanding what they are trying to achieve? How can they know what they are trying to achieve without fully understanding their definition of success? Once they have understood this, they can begin to answer the question about success that launches the next chapter.

✅ Key Takeaways

1. From an early age, we are given different labels which can create in us a victim mentality.
2. By comparing their current selves to the future selves they wish to be, students begin to map out the personal attributes they wish to possess.
3. The large majority of our fears and worries stem from things we cannot control. We can only control our response to the challenging moments in life.

☁ Points to Ponder—Chapter 5

1. Do you carry with you any victimizing labels?
2. Knowing your demographic of students, what labels and worries might they possess?

6

Defining Success

Guiding Students to Their Authentic Definition

Bowl Meeting: What Is Your Definition of Success?

What is your definition of success? This question is the crux of this book. How can you have a success-filled life if you are not sure what success means to you? To define what success is, authentically and personally, takes time. It takes sampling the fruits of life and finding out what is bitter and what is not. Yet, the journey to obtaining success begins by first seeking out your definition. Society pigeonholes us into thinking fame and fortune is the be-all and end-all of existence. Those are the ultimate symbols of success—at least according to what we see portrayed in countless TV programs.

This is a leading misconception that students and even many adults have to overcome. Fame and fortune can be indicators of success, but tragically, as we have witnessed with many famous people, those two elements alone do not lead to a fulfilled life.

When you are passionate about something, it is difficult to not talk about it. Take for example, a dinner I enjoyed recently

DOI: 10.4324/9781003374497-6

with my friend, Kevan. Kevan is a muscular six foot, seven tall, with a beautiful blonde wife and two (very tall) children. At the time we had dinner, he was finishing up renovations on his lakefront home. He is a good father, husband, and salesman. I have rarely been around him when he hasn't been laughing and in a good mood.

Through our dinner conversation, I discussed the topics in this book and how I share them with my students. At three different points, Kevan mentioned how much he enjoyed his job. However, each time he qualified that statement by saying, "But I know it is not as fulfilling as your job," meaning my job as a teacher. The third time he said it, I stopped him and asked, "Then what can you do that would make you feel fulfilled?" I added that our jobs don't have to be our passion or even our purpose. After further discussion, he laughed and said, "This is my homework, isn't it?" I laughed and replied, "Yes, it is."

Kevan lives what many would see as a great and rewarding life. Yet, like so many of us, there might be one small element missing that could take that life and make it amazing! Without reflecting on our definition of success, how can we ever get it to that level? The message of defining success resonates beyond the borders of a classroom, but it can start within those borders.

When asked, "How do you define success?" learners' initial answers typically revolve around a good family, a good house, and a good job. If you look at them individually, you will notice each one of those answers requires further examination. Does a good family involve kids? Do you just need to pay your bills, or do you want to have money to travel? How big is a nice house? What will determine if you are happy at your job? When will you know you are successful?

We owe it to our learners to help them define and understand their personal meaning of success. As I have touched on briefly, it is important to get students away from thinking success equals money or money equals success. The two are often connected, but it is more important to emphasize success will be accomplished by bringing value to the table. There are many wealthy individuals who have still not felt accomplished.

More than Money

Thus, money is not the definition of success. It can be just one indication of success. Success leaves clues. While money can be one, so can fame, influence, impact, or good health. Therefore, the definition of success needs to address multiple facets of life, such as financial, family, social, spiritual, emotional, intellectual, physical, and career. By defining what success means in all those areas, learners can set goals to accomplish said success. It is important to remember, if any of these areas fall short of a person's ultimate goal of success, it can lead to the feeling of failure.

The chart shown in Figure 6.1 depicts one example of how the facets of success can be dissected. A person might designate more of the chart to a particular facet or add/eliminate a slice. The definition of success will alter over time, as will the facets and their portion. Shifts occur in life that change a person's passion, desires, knowledge, and skillset. This is to be anticipated, especially when it comes to younger learners, who will have exposure to unique experiences that will alter their definitions.

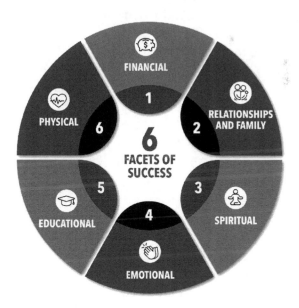

FIGURE 6.1 Here is one visual representation of the facets of success.

Also, people may define success by what they feel is absent or lacking from their lives. For all these reasons, it is important to not only have them analyze their current definition of success, but to instill in them a general understanding of how to obtain success. The great thing is, as I have mentioned, since success leaves clues it means it can be learned and to some extent duplicated.

Throughout all these lessons, questions, and discussions, I continually challenge learners to think about these things:

1. Is success completely dependent upon money?
2. Can you achieve success without first having a goal?
3. Can you achieve a lot of things without feeling successful?
4. Who determines when you are successful?

My goal is to guide them to an understanding that there are many facets of success and if any one of them is underdeveloped, the likelihood that they will feel unsuccessful is greatly increased. At this point, I introduce to them the graphic aid Figure 6.2 (this is also found in Appendix G).

I give them time to write down each facet they would need to feel successful in each of these areas. I stress that if one area is not important to them, then they should skip it. They can also add another area to the graph. For my purposes, I have them discuss career under finances and education. This way they can start to see the overlap of many of these facets and stress the importance of education. This information is taped in the back of their notebooks, to be used later for their time capsule.

What follows in Figure 6.3 is an example of one student's work. This is just a snippet, but it allows you to see how the students can become reflective through the activity.

The old adage, "You never learn something until you have to teach it," resonates with me as it applies to this lesson. By focusing my brain to compartmentalize my life into facets of success, it has allowed me to truly traverse some difficult waters. As previously mentioned, in December of 2019, my mother died suddenly of a heart attack. She had no prior heart conditions, so the family was floored by the rapidity of this event.

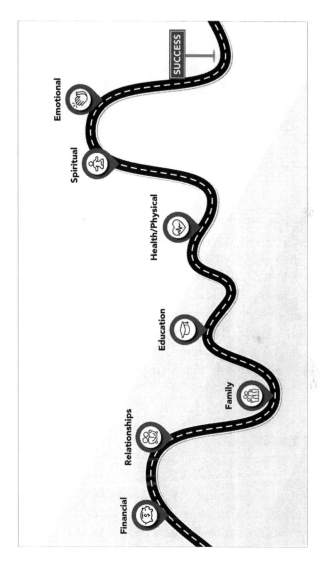

FIGURE 6.2 Facets of success road map.

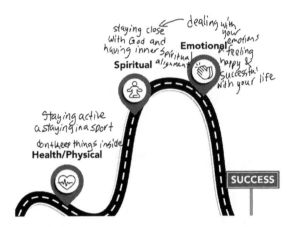

FIGURE 6.3 This demonstrates a student's reflection on the facets of success map.

Then, within two months, my brother-in-law called to say my sister had been rushed to the hospital with a horrible respiratory issue. She spent five days in the intensive care unit (thankfully, she recovered). But you can imagine how reminiscent that was of the earlier situation with my mother. At that moment, my "family" facet of success was at a low point—the lowest point it had ever been. During the months surrounding both events, had I not been teaching my students about the facets of success, it would have been extremely easy for me, emotionally, to slip into a rather dark slump.

Measuring Success

However, since I had been so focused on the concept that success is composed of multiple areas, I was able to identify other areas of my life, such as work and magic, that were going tremendously well. This allowed (and still allows) me to handle the grief. I shared a previous personal reflection with my students. To me, it is important for them to understand I am implementing in my own life what I am teaching them, as well as the value of creating their own working definition of success, especially when life throws trials at them.

Once they have identified generalized goals for each facet, I introduce to them the facets of success chart. Let me first deconstruct my chart and then share with you examples of how I teach this, along with a student example.

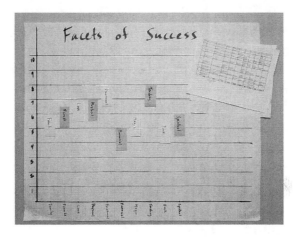

FIGURE 6.4 This is an image of my facets of success chart. In the upper right corner is the rubric.

Figure 6.4 is an image of a chart that hangs in one of my rooms in my house. On the left-hand side it is numbered one through ten. The sticky notes are my ten facets of success. They are family, friends, love, physical, emotional, financial, magic, teaching, book, and spiritual. For me, those are the categories of my life that I need to be healthy in order to feel successful.

In the upper right-hand corner is a rubric. This tells me how I can move up from a two to a three in friends or from a five to a six in finances, and so on. In essence, those are my goals for each facet. In the bottom left is where I just write down the date and the total of all my facets. What I love so much about this is chart is that it offers a tangible way to interact with your goals. Sometimes they move up. Sometimes they move down. Far too often, people are told to write down their goals, but then what happens? They never look at them again. This chart gives you a way to track your goals on a regular basis.

In addition, it allows you to visually see the facets that are "high" or doing well in your life, and the ones that might need some attention. The visual element of this is crucially important. When life throws challenges your way—which it invariably will—you can look at your facets of success chart and see that not all areas of your life are low. This can keep you emotionally grounded and keep you from falling into a psychological abyss.

As previously mentioned, 2019 was a very challenging year for me. If I had not been actively teaching this concept to my students and thoroughly embracing the concept of multiple facets of success, any one of those challenges could have spiraled me downward into a low emotional state. However, I was able to continually remind myself that despite my grief and personal pain, magic and teaching were going well. Even though other categories such as my physical and emotional health were low, I was still able to cling to the higher facets and work to heal the low-lying ones.

Implementing the Chart

When teaching the facets of success to my students, I have them start off by creating a rubric for five categories: physical, emotional, friends, family, and school. As a class, we walk through the levels together. I know where I want it to go, but I solicit feedback from them to obtain increased "buy-in" from the students. The final product looks similar to Table 6.1.

Throughout the process, I continually remind them that this has to be personalized. They must reflect on each category and what each step means to them. For the family facet, it will look very different for each person. I left the school facet blank on purpose. They must fill it in based on their current self-evaluation of academic progress. This can include grades, test scores, quality of work, or any other milestones they wish to accomplish academically. Once we finish, I then challenge them to add in a facet that is unique to them. It could be centered on a hobby, such as playing a musical instrument, or a sport such as basketball.

As they create the rubric for their charts, the bottom rung—or number one on the chart—would be their lowest area. Take for example, the emotional category. Hopefully, they are not starting

TABLE 6.1

Example of a facet of success rubric.

	Physical	Emotional	Friends	Family	School
5	Exercise 3x a week Eat Right Feel Great!	Conquering and vibrant! No matter what comes your way, you are ready.	Two friends who nourish and inspire you	Great! High Level of communication, Listening and enjoying each other's company.	
4	Exercise 2x a week Good eating	Vibrant! Those around you recognize you are a beacon of positive light.	One friend who nourishes and inspires you	Good with parents and siblings. Growing communication skills Growing honor and respect.	
3	Exercise 1x a week Improved diet	Good. You recognize life is what you make of it	Good, but not deep	Decent with parents and siblings. Some level of communication.	
2	Exercise 1x a week Poor diet	Sluggish. Emotionally Drained. No Inspiration.	Looking for deeper friendships	Improved with parents but poor with siblings	
1	Inactive Poor Diet	Depressed	Not seeking to nurture relationships	Poor relationship with parents and siblings	

at a number one: depression. However, they want to include what, in their minds, would be the lowest for that category. I challenge them to create the chart where they start off at a two or three and work their way up to a five. Once they do, they create a new rubric. Once they complete the rubric, then they build the facets of success chart in their notebooks. There is nothing overly complicated about it. It can all fit on one page in their notebook.

At this point, the learner is on their way to building a successful life, but it takes more than just a chart to get them there. It takes more of the right questions and deeper reflection on their part. One way I frame a further discussion on success with my students is by introducing the following engineering design challenge. I include this because of the ease in implementing it and because of the tangible representation it creates for the learners.

To begin, I give students a piece of paper, five index cards, and a strip of tape from the table to the floor. The challenge is to design and build a table that can support as many textbooks as possible. The legs have to be attached to the table and cannot be taped to the surface on which it sits. Every year it blows my students' minds how many books the paper table can hold—that is, if they design it well. Sure, there are groups that have bizarre designs with accordion-type legs or cylinders turned on their sides like wheels that do not support even one book. However, that paper can support way more than initially imagined!

Guess what happens to the groups when I allow them to redesign their tables after they have seen successful examples? As you would expect, the number of successful tables grows in leaps and bounds. With a properly designed support system and a little knowledge, the students achieve success. Just like the paper table, success in general must be built with the correct support system.

There is no one recipe for success. This is why a person's facets of success chart will be unique. However, there are common attributes shared by people successful in life. Regardless of the definition of success, these four items are always present, supporting their accomplishments. Turn to Chapter 7 to learn more details about each one.

✓ Key Takeaways

1. Success requires balancing all the areas in our lives we deem necessary to be successful.
2. After students define their specific facets of success, they must track their progress to stay on track.
3. Having students create an authentic facets of success chart is the most important content item in this book.

💭 Points to Ponder—Chapter 6

1. What is a unique facet of success that you possess?
2. What facet do you think your students will overlook the most?

7

Four-Legged Foundation

The Main Components Students Need to Ensure Success

By now, you may be wondering: is this guy serious? Or does he just like cheesy illustrations? Trust me. As tacky as this idea may sound, if you do this activity and connect it to success, you will have reference points you can always reflect on during the entire year. Plus, the learners will not forget it. As with any table, if any of the four legs are removed the table is worthless, yet in combination with each other they offer incredible strength.

Leg 1: Value

The first leg is value. It's crucial. My favorite question for a Bowl Meeting regarding this first essential is:

Bowl Meeting: What Value Do You Bring to the Table?

Here, let me tell you about Lleyton. Lleyton is one of the most brilliant students I have ever had the privilege of teaching. He actually scored thirty-four on the ACT (twenty-one is considered competitive) in seventh grade, which would have been high

DOI: 10.4324/9781003374497-7

enough right then to get him into any college. I was fortunate enough to teach him in my STEM class all three years of middle school.

The summer prior to his junior year of high school we crossed paths again when he worked as a teaching assistant in a training seminar I facilitated. Since his goal was to get into the Massachusetts Institute of Technology (MIT), I asked him, "What value do you bring to the table?" and encouraged him to write these qualities down. He quickly produced an accurate and lengthy list of adjectives, such as the ability to collaborate, facilitate, communicate, and brainstorm. These are such important skills that every student/adult should have, so by no means did I downplay these skills. But I warned him every applicant to MIT will say something similar.

Then, I asked, "What have you done, or are you doing, to prove you can do those things?" Trust me, he had done a lot, like participating in academic and athletic teams. However, I wanted him to recognize that those things, when aligned with his goal, added value to him. That's when I challenged him over the next two years to continue to add value to himself so he would knock the socks off the folks at MIT. I am so excited to see where his future leads! As brilliant as a student might be, they still need to understand how the value they bring to the table plays a significant role in their success. (By the way, Lleyton did wind up going to MIT.)

Success on so many levels is not just thinking about, "What makes me happy?" It is aligning what you do that makes you happy to the end user. In the example of my former student Lleyton, he was deeply involved in rowing for his high school. This made him well-rounded and happy. The end user (in this case, the people at MIT) could see how he took leadership roles and proved he was outgoing by being involved in this sport. Therefore, as previously mentioned, sports can have value.

Lleyton was also involved with the robotics team. This too is something he enjoyed, but it added value to himself (in comparison to others) for the end user. Keeping the end user or the end goal in mind can help students navigate what activities are providing value to them. The end users are going to be looking for evidence that the students possess value. Essentially, I challenge students to look for evidence in their lives that proves they add value. If learners make a conscious effort to look at what they have already done and make a conscious effort to plan for more ways to add value to themselves, then they are progressing toward their personal definition of success.

Focusing on the Goal

This resonates throughout all the facets of success. Take for example, relationship success. If individuals think about their actions and how they benefit themselves and the other person involved in the relationship, they are more likely to achieve the long-term success needed to maintain that relationship. In this case, they are thinking about the other person as the end user. I realize this is a mechanical way of phrasing this, but the message remains the same. A learner will gain success by adding value to themselves that aligns with their end goal or user.

Once learners can understand that success comes from bringing value to the table, they can begin to understand where education plays a part in success. I use "education" in the broad sense. Perhaps it would be better if I use the word "learning." Hopefully, a learner can connect value in what they are learning to their passion. If others find value in what a student provides, and what that learner provides aligns with their passion, then jackpot! They can make a living doing the thing they love.

Earl Nightingale, the successful broadcaster, life coach, and speaker I mentioned earlier, described three things that must be contemplated when assessing a person's value to a field. These three questions can help guide students to a decision about whether their passion is worth pursuing.

1. Is there a demand for what we do? Meaning by adding value to their passion, does this place them in a "high needs" category?

2. How well do we do what we do? They might be pursuing a passion in a field that is in high need, but what is their ability level in that field?
3. How difficult is it to replace us? Can someone be trained to do what they do in just a matter of weeks?

Learners need to reflect on these questions to see if they are adding value and if they want to pursue a career following their passion. It is important to remember the value a person brings to the table is not gained overnight. Instead, it is developed over time by continually learning and honing a craft.

Another great example of adding value occurred when I crossed paths with another former student of mine, Landon. As a junior in high school, instead of taking the typical dual-enrollment courses at a local college, Landon opted to take courses to obtain a certification in mechatronics. This multidisciplinary field deals with things like robotics, control systems, and electro-mechanical systems—truly the wave of the future. This will give him the ability to go into college full time and have strong background in a field he really enjoys.

> "You may not be able to do all you find out, but make sure you find out all you CAN do."
> —Jim Rohn [1]

Jim Rohn was an author, life coach, and motivational speaker who launched his speaking career in 1963. I am going to summarize many of his concepts here about adding value. He mentions that if your definition of success is wealth, then you study wealth. If it is health, then you study health. If it is happiness, or spirituality, then study those things. Value is added by being a lifelong learner of a topic. For students to gain success, they need to know the correlation between value and success. Rohn once noted that income does not exceed personal development. He meant that the more developed and educated we are as individuals, the more likely it is that our income will increase. This is one of the many reasons why lottery winners, celebrities, and professional athletes go broke so frequently. They do not focus on the personal development they need to maintain and grow the large sums of money they possess.

Lottery winners are more likely than the average American to declare bankruptcy within three to five years. What's more, studies have shown that winning the lottery does not necessarily make you happier or healthier.

—CNBC [2]

As the previous example of riches-to-rags demonstrates, adding money to a situation without increasing the value a person adds can lead to failure. This is why adding value is such an important principle for learners to grasp. If individuals wish to succeed in life, they must have a deep understanding of what value they bring to the table as they work harder on self-development.

Taking Inventory

Understanding this first point about bringing value to the table causes the learner to reflect on the skills they already possess. Having this understanding gives a person confidence stepping into a job interview or scholarship interview because they recognize what value they bring.

A follow-up question is: "What value are you adding to yourself today?" Throughout their lives, this question provides for a time of self-evaluation of strengths and weaknesses. It allows for the people to periodically determine what they need to add to themselves now to achieve their goals in the future. This question connects directly back to the question of a person's definition of success and the facets of success chart.

When they have a clear definition of success, a person could look at their current facets and see which one or ones are low. By determining that, they can use the question of what value they are adding to themselves today to infuse time and energy into raising that facet. This is how to achieve and maintain balance.

When I ask students or other learners, "What value do you bring to the table?" many times, they will be a little confused. That is okay. Anticipate this. Relish this. This is when reflection happens. The person must make an authentic self-evaluation to determine what things they are doing in their lives to propel them forward and what things in their lives are holding them back. No one in the history of humankind while on their death bed said, "I wish I had slept more," or "I wish I had played more video games." Regrets come from the moments in life we could have added value to ourselves, but didn't. Teach your learners the importance of adding value to themselves.

Xs and Os

This final example requires the student to perform an eye-opening reflection. I challenge you to walk through this as well. Look at the rudimentary chart displayed in Figure 7.1.

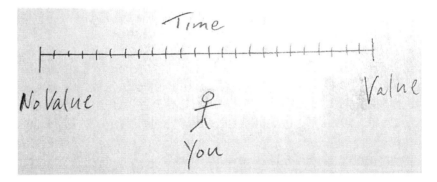

FIGURE 7.1 No value vs. value chart. A quick visual for the students.

To understand its merits, let's walk through the twenty-four hours of the day. Each tick mark represents an hour. Starting on the left side, each hour during the day that value is added, the student can add an "O" on a tick mark. If the student sleeps eight hours, that is adding value; sleep is necessary for healing, growing, and energy. Therefore, they can move eight steps right. That leaves them with sixteen hours to add more value, but if they are sleeping longer than eight hours (unless they are sick or healing), each hour over they have to add an "X." Then, for each activity they perform they can add an "X" or an "O." Spending a quality hour building relationships, exercising, strengthening their mind, or developing a skill earns an "O." Anything else, they get an "X." The daily total can be easily recorded and charted. Over time, being conscientious of the hours of the day can make a world of difference in a person's progress in achieving their definition of success.

When learners authentically walk through this activity evaluating how they spend their time, it is a shocker. I have to be transparent here as well. There are many days I have way too many "Xs" compared to "Os." Having individuals draw this chart and then monitor their time—even if only for a couple days—creates a lot of impact. How much time do the students spend over the weekend or summers that add little to no value to them? Those are the key days when students need to seek out adding value to themselves. Those are also the key times when students can begin to separate themselves from the herd. I emphasize the goal is not to eliminate all the "Xs," but to switch some of them to adding value to themselves. Even if they begin by just adding fifteen minutes more a day of "Os," that time adds up!

Just for clarity, value is added by doing things that help an individual be a better person. That can come in the form of increased health, knowledge, and interpersonal relationships, so marking eating or folding the laundry as adding value is a stretch. Essentially, the daily activities necessary for living aren't adding value to oneself, at least not in this activity.

Now that we've taken an extended look at value, let's move on to leg 2.

Leg 2: Success Demands Sacrifice

The discussion of sacrifice really is a journey through these three key questions:

1. What does sacrifice mean to you?
2. What are you willing to sacrifice now for obtaining your goal later?

3. What are you currently sacrificing to add value to yourself?

When it comes to discussing sacrifice, a Bowl Meeting is initiated by the earlier question:

Bowl Meeting: What Does Sacrifice Mean to You?

When it comes to success, learners have one common misunderstanding. They do not understand success comes from sacrifice. They do not understand that all these celebrities, millionaires, influencers, professional athletes, et cetera et cetera, reached that position through sacrifice.

They had to sacrifice time from their families, friends, video games, partying, junk food, television, social media, sleep, and a million other things to focus on their craft. They gave up immediate gratification for their long-term success. The main question above just prompts the learners to contemplate the meaning of sacrifice. This Bowl Meeting is more about leading them to understand what it means and to be able to recognize it in their lives.

Once we have discussed what sacrifice means to them, I follow up with the question of what they would be willing to sacrifice now to obtain a goal later. Once they have defined sacrifice, this question almost works as a pledge for the learner. This also makes them begin to specifically identify what they can foresee giving up now to get what they want later.

It does not matter how they define their success. They must sacrifice something. If they define success as having a great relationship with a significant other, then they must sacrifice their personal desire to be with their friends all the time. If they define success as having good grades, then they must give up a few hours of video games. The road to success requires hard work. There is no quick "win" or moment that is going to occur and—"bam!"—they are successful. There is no championship athlete who didn't put in the countless hours of hard work. I hate to admit it, but even these people who our students idolize, called influencers, have put in hard work and planning to achieve their status.

While sacrifice is tough, it is necessary:

◆ "But I don't wanna stop playing video games," a student may whine. I tell that person: "If you wish to maintain your GPA and get that scholarship, then you will have to."

◆ "But I don't wanna stop dating him (or her)," some say. Well, they might have to if this other person is not supporting them in their endeavors and only causes the would-be achiever to backslide.

Sacrifice is not easy. That is why it is defined as the destruction or surrender of something for the sake of something else. In many of the definitions of sacrifice, the word "slaughter" is used. I think that provides a graphic image of what is needed for success. You must slaughter the things in your way that do not support your journey to success (figuratively speaking, of course.)

By no means am I encouraging learners to stop participating in sports, clubs, or life. Those are all crucial components to learning their passion, developing transferable skills, and adding value to their lives. However, they need to ponder if the activities they focus on are adding value to their self-development or goal development. If not, then they might need to be sacrificed.

> "Where attention goes, energy flows."
>
> —Tony Robbins [3]

This quote from Robbins is a great reminder that if we focus on the wrong things that are not leading us to our goal or personal growth, we are burning energy—and, more importantly—time. This reminds me of something I stumbled across a few years ago, about a lamenting valedictorian who went viral when giving a speech to his classmates. He bluntly questioned why he was being honored since, in his eyes, he had been trivialized down to a three-digit number. Namely, his grade point average. He continued to discuss how, in order to achieve his valedictorian status, he had to sacrifice many social opportunities offered at the high school level and essentially did not receive as good an "education" as his peers.

This young man was a poignant example how the current model of education neglects self-development in exchange for academic gains. Year after year, he gained educational/academic success, but at the cost of his relational success. He needed ongoing self-evaluation to determine if his pie of success included all the proper ingredients. Everyone should carefully evaluate what they are sacrificing to achieve success and make sure what they are gaining adds value and fulfillment to their definition of success. Learners need to understand a crucial leg needed to support their table of success is sacrifice, but what they sacrifice must align with their ultimate definition of success and add value to their self-development.

When deliberating over the necessity of sacrifice, I love hearing students' working definition of the term. I frequently get answers such as:

◆ "Doing things you don't want to do to get a goal."
◆ "Giving up stuff you normally love ... to achieve something that is more important to you."

One definition I really enjoyed that a student shared:

◆ "Give up something you want for something you need."

I thought the latter observation was quite astute, especially since it came from a seventh-grader. Each of these three examples demonstrates how students can grasp the term of sacrifice. So does this one: "Give up something you love." I thought about that for a moment and realized how this student rang the bell. For example, I do not drink coffee. So, if someone asked me to stop drinking coffee each morning, that wouldn't be a sacrifice. For others, that might be a horrible thing to relinquish. You only sacrifice when you are giving up something you value or trade it for something else.

Before leaving this topic, I have the students reflect on a third question: "What are you currently sacrificing to add value to yourself?" It takes a moment for the students to grasp this idea, but one by one they start sharing what they are giving up to achieve a goal. Many will share how they are sacrificing time from their friends to pursue their passion, be that sports, art, dancing, or something else.

In helping them to internalize this question, I encourage them to sincerely analyze their screen time. This is one of the biggest and easiest time drains students can sacrifice that would free up loads of time for them to add value to themselves. By recognizing that we sacrifice something whenever we devote our time and energy to something else, learners can realize life requires a balancing act.

Leg 3: Success Mandates Self-Discipline

Another Bowl Meeting question that relates to success:

What Does Self-Discipline Mean to You?

We cannot obtain sacrifice without self-discipline. Self-discipline cannot be obtained without sacrifice. In his book *Outliers*, best-selling author Malcolm Gladwell describes the ten-thousand-hour rule [4]. Essentially, Gladwell describes how success in a field requires ten thousand hours of focused, disciplined practice. Regardless of the time involved, focused self-discipline is mandatory for success.

> Self-discipline is the bridge between dreams and reality.

What does self-discipline look like? It is the basketball player shooting one hundred extra free throws at the end of every practice. It is the dancer who practices their routine after everyone has gone home for an additional hour, each and every time. It is the writer who wants to watch the professional volleyball tournament on TV but chooses to write instead because he has designated Saturday mornings for that task. It is the student who refuses to get on social media before finishing their homework. It is consistently passing up those five-hundred-calorie drinks because of a weight-loss goal. Self-discipline is a repeated, defined, and designated behavior essential to success. For each of these examples, I hope you see how sacrifice and self-discipline form a symbiotic relationship. Hopefully, you can formulate the connection between sacrifice and self-discipline for your learners.

The first time I discussed this topic in depth with my students, I simply asked them to share their thoughts on what self-discipline means. I was surprised to learn how many of them had a negative connotation of this quality. Wading further into the discussion, I realized that especially in the school setting, anytime the word "discipline" pops up, it takes on a negative meaning. It dawned on me that I needed to tear down their preconceived notions and get them to realign their working definition. Once we further discussed the concept, they began to realize self-discipline means staying focused even when you are surrounded by distractions from your goal. This was an eye-opening discussion for both me and my students, but it was necessary to ensure their understanding of how self-discipline empowers you to achieve your goal. Once they grasp that self-discipline is a repeated, defined, and designated behavior essential to gaining success, then you can move forward with the discussion.

This Bowl Meeting has two crucial follow-up questions that typically grow organically out of the discussion:

1. In what ways do you currently show you are self-disciplined?
2. In what areas do you wish you had more self-discipline?

I love these two questions because they put learners in reflection mode again. They must look in the mirror and evaluate their strengths and weaknesses. Figure 7.2 shows a few answers I have received in classes. Teaching virtually and face-to-face during the pandemic allowed me to capture student responses shared during our Bowl Meetings. You will see these examples sprinkled throughout the book

9:47 AM

I am self disciplined in baton and school. At baton
I also wish I had more because I easily want to
stop and hang around when I should be doing
stuff. Sometimes for school, I just don't want to
do homework.

9:47 AM

I wish i was more disciplined in health, like to
make better choice with eating and working out.
I also want more motivation to get schoolwork
and other things done.

9:47 AM

I self-discipline myself at school by getting good
grades. I wish I was more self-disciplined with my
behavior with my parents.

FIGURE 7.2 Student reflections on self-discipline.

As you can see from Figure 7.2, the students do a good job of
analyzing themselves. Those responses came in the midst of the
pandemic. Even on a virtual platform, these questions can elicit
deep reflection from the learners. The more open your students
get in Bowl Meetings, the more they share. Take this student's
response to the same two questions.

9:47 AM

What i currently show self-discipline, when i get
angry i don't start yelling at the person. What i
need disciplined in is not to hurt my self on purpose.

FIGURE 7.3 This student was extremely transparent about their reflection on self-discipline.

Wow! When you get responses like Figure 7.3, be ready to
think fast. In this circumstance, I quickly private messaged her
in the virtual meeting and asked her about it. Then, I immediately contacted my school's S.A.F.E. coordinator, who handles
situations like this. She followed up and found out the situation

was under control. But be ready—these discussions can lead to students being thoroughly transparent.

Before leaving the topic of self-discipline, I must mention Inky Johnson, who has one of the most amazing stories regarding discipline and success. Inky was a standout college football player, destined for the NFL. His dream to be a professional football player was not centered on fame and fortune, but a desire to get his family out of their impoverished circumstances. Just a few college games away from achieving his dream, tragedy struck. He suffered a life-changing injury that brought his football career to a screeching halt: a hit that caused serious nerve damage to his right arm. Knowing he would never play football again, he disciplined himself physically and mentally for the journey that lay ahead. From that point, he has become an amazing motivational speaker and author. One of his quotes resonates frequently throughout my mind:

> "The harder you work, the harder it is to surrender."
> —Inky Johnson [5]

Inky's message says it all. The harder we toil over a goal, the more likely that we will never give up on that goal. Surrender is not an option. If we put sweat-inducing work and effort into our education, jobs, hobbies, relationships, and entrepreneurial enterprises, then we are unlikely to wave the white flag of defeat. There is no reason why you can't discuss such things with your students or learners.

Leg 4: Motivation!

The reality of this leg prompts the Bowl Meeting question:

What Motivates You to Succeed in School and Life?

I would hate to describe motivation as the most important of the four legs, but without it, the other three legs wouldn't exist. Motivation is the *WHY?* If someone has their motivation loosely formuiated, barely articulated, or scarcely expressed, they face little hope of success. A clearly defined "why?" is what forces you to get up in the morning, even on your day off. A vividly defined "why?" is what keeps you working late into the night or missing meals without even realizing it. This is why when students or learners face the question: *What motivates you to succeed in school or life?* they must give it some serious reflection.

This question prompts additional follow-up questions to get them to narrow their answer. Is it their desire to please parents, please teachers, fear of failure, the need for recognition, the need to be significant, make an impact, earn money, or gain fame? Try to get them to define what it is, but through this process remember there is no wrong answer here. It is all based on their own reflection. This answer might unravel over time. It also might require some vulnerability on their part. Therefore, they might not choose to share too openly in a large group setting.

Then, there is a more difficult question: Where does that motivation come from? A coach, parents, friends, or teachers? Or does it come from within? As mentioned, for years I felt driven, but I didn't know my destination. That is an awful feeling. While I was motivated to learn, I didn't know how and where to apply it. For years and years, I did not think about the way I think. However, it finally struck me: I am motivated by the need to be significant. Not to be famous or even rich, but the need to know I made (and am making) a difference.

For so long, I thought I needed to be an astronaut to have such an impact. I had yet to realize the tremendous impact I was having as an educator; it took me a long time to grasp that reality. This is partially why I am sharing these words with you. Additionally, my fear for students is that relying on others for motivation at this early stage in life will fail. More accurately, they will fail because one day that extrinsic motivator will not be there to fan that flame of motivation. Then what? They quit? They fall on their face? Curl up and suck their thumb? This is why it is so important to define what intrinsically motivates them and to develop this resource.

Searching for Inspiration

Excitement is easy to create, but inspiration is difficult.

By no means am I devaluing extrinsic motivators. Short-term motivation to succeed can be sparked by others and at times is necessary. Coaches, parents, friends, and teachers can all be great sources of motivation. However, to fan that flame into inspiration, it has to come from an intrinsic force within. They must think about their driving force or inspiration and discover how to internalize it. It should be a constant pull, meaning their motivation is pulling them to complete their goal. They are pulled to get out of bed early to work on their success plan.

If the ice-cream truck turned down this street, people would get excited. But inspiration begins with a spark that turns into a flame that engulfs your spirit (and lasts long after the ice-cream truck leaves your neighborhood).

To reach that point, students must understand themselves. For me, success is coupled with motivation. One major component of my definition of success is based on my motivation, since personally they are quite interdependent. For others, there might be a clear distinction between the two.

Let me explain what I mean. For me, clarity didn't arrive until I was able to define my motivation. My definition of success is making an impact on others in a positive, significant way. My "why?" is because I wish to empower people to think deeper, fail forward, and create a personalized definition of success. So, my motivation boils down to my intrinsic desire to significantly impact others' lives. As I mentioned before, this is not to have my name in lights, but to have impacted others in a way that positively directs their lives.

Hopefully, you can see how success and motivation can be joined together at the hip. Often, there is an emotional reason for someone's motivation. In fact, sincere, intrinsic motivation will always have some emotional tie to it. For example, a student might define success as having a home and making a living where they can provide for their family. This could be a deep-seated motivation because they now live in poverty.

What Do I Say Now?

Here is a particular example of how one's motivation and definition of success can have significant emotional ties to them. One time, while discussing their definitions of success, a student in my class shared, "I define success by my dad accepting me as his son." What?! Seriously, what was I supposed to say to that? In my mind I was thinking, "I am not prepared for this; you are supposed to say a home or a nice car!"

After fumbling for words, I redirected the question by saying, "So that is important to you?" I was just trying to buy time to think of something to say. Granted, he shared this knowing it would be read aloud, so he wanted to talk about it. But I know my limitations as a teacher; no way was I going to walk down that dark alleyway. I followed up again and said, "Even if you get a great job, a house, and a good family, will you not feel successful without that (your father's approval)?"

"No," he replied.

"I hope you get it one day then," I said before moving on and submitting his name to the school counselor. Listen, I know how much weight I can handle and that was way too heavy for me. Therefore, be prepared for an occasional strong emotional tie to a student's motivation or definition of success. In this student's case, there is a bright update. At the time he wrote the above definition of success he was in seventh grade. I had the privilege of teaching him in eighth grade as well. The next time he answered the question about success this way: "Success is having a stable job, a source of income, food, a house, and a dog." My heart leaped when I read those words. I followed up and asked him how things were with his father; he said they had made major improvements.

Sometimes a person can have more than one form of motivation. For me, another one stems from my childhood. As I shared earlier, my father working nearly around the clock triggered a strong motivation for me to work hard, but also strive for more balance in life. I share my personal reflections with you as a way to show you more examples of how these Bowl Meeting questions may appear as simplistic on the surface, yet, they can have some deep-rooted responses.

How Can I Power Up?

When it comes to motivation, the greatest follow-up question is, "What happens when motivation dwindles?" This is a tough question, and the answer is different for everyone. However, I can pose some suggestions. One way to power up your motivation is by surrounding yourself with like-minded people who share your passion. When the conversations and discussions are enlightening, motivating, and empowering around your passion, motivation comes naturally. Surrounding yourself with the right people who challenge you to be better than you already are can lead to continued gains in your ultimate goal.

While there are a number of negatives about social media, especially its endless atmosphere of comparison, it also offers a major benefit. If you can't find someone who shares your passion locally, then social media can link you to others around the nation (even the world). Still, I strongly suggest seeking out face-to-face conversations. Passion can be contagious, and way more contagious when transmitted in person. Plus, these conversations can lead to brainstorming and the birth of new ideas. On top of that, they can launch new areas to explore and exciting opportunities.

In writing this book, the inevitability of writer's block loomed around every corner. When it reared its ugly head, I started inundating myself with all kinds of podcasts or YouTube videos bursting with motivational messages. I dove into books or articles that coincided with my topic. It was not uncommon that I sparked conversations, often with strangers, about some of the questions I have posed throughout this book. Their responses led to writing points. Of course, the greatest source of inspiration came from talking to my students. Many a time, smack dab in the middle of a conversation, I would run over to my desk to write down ideas that sprang from our discussions. (You would think by then I would have just carried a notepad with me.)

If a learner's passion is performance-based, like sports or the performing arts, then they can seek out a more experienced person. Advise learners to study these people. Talk to them. Figure out what makes them tick. If they have the time, start training with them or playing against them. It can make students more engaged and give them that extra driving force. Though sometimes more easily recognizable in performance-based passions, this advice is apropos in all areas. Remember Noah, that student-turned-magician, I told you about in Chapter 4? He is great in this sphere. He has no fear and thus has established great relationships with many other magicians. He does not hesitate to ask them to teach him something. Couple that with his own motivation and he has made tremendous growth in a short time.

If none of these suggestions work, tell learners that it might be time to reevaluate their goals in the first place. If the motivation is not there, perhaps it is not something they truly desire to accomplish. They then need to evaluate if their motivation matches their goals. Their mind might try to tell them one thing but their heart another. Perhaps something could be waiting in the wings that they are more passionate about.

Look at my example of being an astronaut. That dream is still in there, but a louder, more vivid dream has taken its place: Once published, I want this book to get into the hands of fifty thousand teachers. If only 40% of them read this book and implement or teach just one lesson from it, that will impact millions of students.

Check my math here. Let's pretend those twenty thousand teachers are middle school or high school teachers and they teach approximately one hundred and fifty students a day. If they teach one of these lessons for five years, then fifteen million students will have a chance at a much more successful and fulfilled life! That sounds lofty, but Florida alone has more than one hundred and eighty thousand teachers. This is an achievable goal. This is why one of the key components to ensuring success and maintaining a high level of motivation is picking a task that is greater than yourself. When we do something that serves a bigger purpose than just a small accomplishment for ourselves, we will be pulled to achieve that goal.

Master Your Morning

Advise learners that if motivation is dwindling, they should evaluate what could be stealing their motivation. Often, it is what they are putting into their brain; what we put into our minds often affects us unknowingly. This is why establishing a good morning routine, one full of motivation to start the day, is exponentially beneficial to obtaining a growth mindset and achieving a personal definition of success.

One of the best ways to start the morning is by hopping out of bed and then making the bed. What a great way to start your day—by already accomplishing something! Retired four-star admiral, William H. McRaven—at one time considered for secretary of defense—wrote a best-selling book in 2017 called *Make Your Bed: Little Things That Can Change Your Life...And Maybe the World*. His famous saying is, "If you want to change the world, start off by making your bed [6]." That is a great point. At least then, at the end of the day, you will come home to a made bed.

The next way to master your morning is to stay off your phone, for as long as you can. There are far too many distractions and ways that the information gleamed from your phone can suck your morning and motivation dry. Whether it be the news or some form of social media, your phone almost has a mystical power to snap you out of the focused state you need to be in to succeed. If you multiply this by 365 days a year, no wonder people's outlook on the world is so dim and their motivation is swirling down the commode.

The most important thing for me is listening to something motivational in the morning. I like to listen to a podcast or YouTube videos, which ensure my mind stays in a growth mindset. Some of my favorites are sales guru Tony Robbins, motivational speaker Les Brown—who coined the phrase, "It's possible" to encourage people to follow their dreams—and Rob Dial, an e-commerce entrepreneur, coach, and host of the *Mindset*

In addition to that always pushing me to be better acedemiclly and also being a better person you have taught me and helped me See maybe a glimpse of my future by knowing my passion and turning it in to a Carrer.

FIGURE 7.4 This reflection emphasizes the importance of discussing their futures with them.

Mentor podcast. Your choices may differ, but the point is to start your day by fanning the flames of motivation instead of dousing them with negativity.

Steps to Powering up Motivation!
1. Collaborate with a peer on social media.
2. Collaborate with a peer in person.
3. Read, watch, and listen to books, videos, and podcasts on the topic.
4. Find a mentor or someone to emulate and learn from.
5. Re-evaluate if goals match with heart and mind.
6. Master your morning.

A key point to emphasize to learners about motivation is that you are not there to motivate them; you are there to educate them, to point and guide them to the motivation inside them. Motivation must come from within themselves (Figure 7.4).

Motivation: Implementation

To make the task as user-friendly as possible, what follows are some "crib notes" for teaching this lesson on motivation. Keep in mind that the goal is to get the learners to grasp where they get their motivation and how to find more.

1. Review the paper table legs of success with your students (if this is how you implemented the other lessons).
2. Have them respond to the following question: What motivates you in life and school?
3. Explain to them the difference between extrinsic and intrinsic motivation. If someone gives them a punishment or reward, it is extrinsic—for example, parents bribing them or punishing them to get good grades. Intrinsic means they do it because they know that is right. They earn good grades because they have future goals in life they wish to accomplish.
4. Now, have them answer the question: Where does your motivation come from? This is when they begin to make the connection between extrinsic and intrinsic. At this point, if you have been having Bowl lessons with the students, they are primed to be reflective. These two examples really showcase the growth in the student's reflection … AND how transparent they will be as shown in Figure 7.5.
5. Finally, you can discuss with them the ways in which they can find greater motivation.

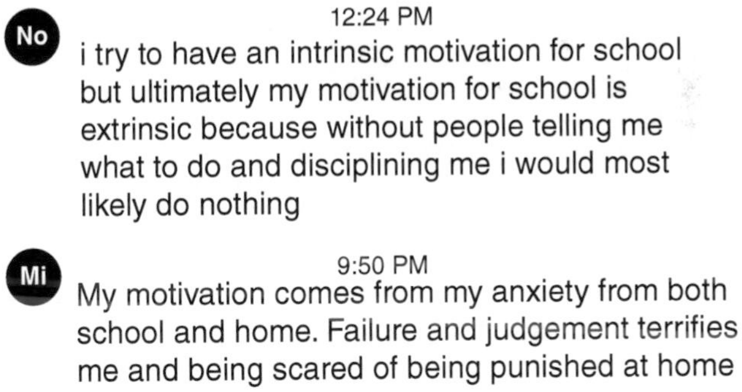

No 12:24 PM
i try to have an intrinsic motivation for school but ultimately my motivation for school is extrinsic because without people telling me what to do and disciplining me i would most likely do nothing

Mi 9:50 PM
My motivation comes from my anxiety from both school and home. Failure and judgement terrifies me and being scared of being punished at home

FIGURE 7.5 These students discuss their motivation.

Believe it or not, all that information can be shared in just one class period. To refer back to the paper table design challenge, when my students complete it, the most successful designs contain a minimum of four legs. Some students try one big round cylinder in the middle, which can support some books—depending on how they built it—but this creation has never supported the most. Some groups choose to make more than four legs, which is equally effective. Regardless of how many legs their table has, if one of the main support legs collapses, the whole table falls.

The same can be said about these four "legs" of success: value, sacrifice, self-discipline, and motivation. If one of them collapses, the person will not obtain or maintain success. This is a very visual analogy for students that can help drive this message home.

✅ Key Takeaways

1. We all need to continually reflect on what value we currently possess and what value we are currently adding to ourselves.
2. Success in any endeavor requires sacrifice. Determining what we sacrifice can be challenging.
3. Self-discipline leads to consistency. Consistency leads to success.
4. Motivation can wax and wane. Finding the source of motivation can propel students to greater success.

💭 Points to Ponder—Chapter 7

1. How do you find motivation when it dwindles?
2. What morning routine do you possess that could be detrimental?
3. What technique do you currently use to motivate your students?

References

1. "Jim Rohn Quotes," *QuoteFancy*, https://quotefancy.com/quote/838071/Jim-Rohn-You-may-not-be-able-to-do-all-you-find-out-but-make-sure-you-find-out-all-you#:~:text=Jim%20Rohn%20Quote%3A%20%E2%80%9CYou%20may,out%20all%20you%20can%20do.%E2%80%9D, accessed August 5, 2021.

2. Abigail Johnson Hess, "Here's why lottery winners go broke," *CBNC*, August 25, 2017, https://www.cnbc.com/2017/08/25/heres-why-lottery-winners-go-broke.html

3. Team Tony, "Where Focus Goes, Energy Flows," *TonyRobbins.com*, https://www.tonyrobbins.com/career-business/where-focus-goes-energy-flows/, accessed August 9, 2021.

4. Malcolm Gladwell, *Outliers: The Story of Success* (New York: Back Bay Books, 2011), 35.

5. Inky Johnson, "The harder you work … the harder it is to surrender!" *Facebook*, November 17, 2017, https://www.facebook.com/watch/?v=1965178480161207

6. William H. McRaven, *Make Your Bed: Little Things That Can Change Your Life…And Maybe the World* (New York: Grand Central Publishing, 2017).

8

Drain or Gain

Determining What Is Impacting Students' Emotional Health

When the academic world and many other venues shifted to a virtual environment in the spring of 2020, I jumped at the chance to create a new, virtual magic show. I wanted to help give people a sense of normalcy and a chance to build community within their businesses. Most of the individuals who hired me in 2020 were representatives from businesses or corporations. However, that changed in January 2021. A college booked me to perform a virtual magic show with a message I have developed over the years in my life and classroom.

When I finished that performance, I was almost in tears. Little did I know my goal that had been crafted years ago—to be able to share magic and my message with people and students outside my classroom—would come to fruition through the virtual realm. Since then, I have performed for multiple colleges and their students. You have already read two of the three questions that I discuss with them:

- What is your definition of success?
- What value do you bring to the table?
- What are you doing to be emotionally successful?

DOI: 10.4324/9781003374497-8

While I have discussed the first two questions in detail, the third one is crucial to achieving and maintaining success.

Bowl Meeting: What Are You Doing to Be Emotionally Successful?

We can have all the money and fame in the world, but if we do not feel emotionally successful, then it will all be for nothing. I discuss the topic of emotions throughout this book. It crops up regularly because of the necessity of tending the garden of our emotions. Based on the discussions I have had with multiple colleges, in this chapter I will look at five areas in a person's life that can either drain or gain their emotions. These areas are quite sneaky; without purposeful reflection, they can have immense impact.

Drain or Gain

Music

Music holds tremendous power over us. Its nostalgic power can instantaneously teleport us back to specific moments in our lives, or change our mood from energetic to sad—all at the tapping of an iPhone link or an online click. In a 2019 article in *Psychology Today*, author Dr. Shahram Heshmat—a retired professor who specializes in behaviors underlying addictions and obesity—points out how we can begin to mimic the emotions expressed in the music: "Listeners mirror their reactions to what the music expresses, such as sadness from sad music, or cheer from happy music. Similarly, ambient music affects shoppers' and diners' moods [1]."

The mimicking Dr. Heshmat describes could be good, bad, or indifferent to our emotions. I have a personal example of this occurrence. In high school, I loved R&B (rhythm and blues) music. If you are unfamiliar with the genre, it is all about love. Everything, from the pursuit to the breakup, is covered by R&B music. My wheelhouse in that genre revolved around artists like Jodeci, Boyz II Men, and Keith Sweat.

One time, I had a buddy over at my house listening to this music. After a little while, he asked, "Is this what you listen to all the time?" A bit proud of my music selection, I quickly responded, "Yes." His quick retort has resonated with me ever since: "No wonder you are lovesick all the time."

If I could play a glass shattering sound effect for you right now, I would. That was what it was like. He was 100% correct. Since I constantly filled my brain with thoughts and emotions derived from music, they wound up becoming a tremendous focus of my high school years. I had no clue how much it was impacting my emotions. I can guarantee that neither do your learners. This is why they need to take thorough stock of what they are listening to, and evaluate how it impacts their emotions.

Friends

The term "friend" has been significantly devalued in recent decades. It has taken on more of the meaning of a vast collection of acquaintances (i.e., as on Facebook or Instagram) rather than an intimate relationship with a small group of people. So, for our definition, I am referring to the people we spend the most time with. Jim Rohn taught me the concept that we are the average of our five closest friends.

If that is the case, how are they influencing you? How are you influencing them? If we see ourselves in our own reflection in the mirror, then what do our friends reflect about us? How are they supporting us? How are we supporting them? I love the standard: Do your friends nourish and inspire you? Do you nourish and inspire them? That is a very high standard, but if they are going to be given the trust to impact our lives, emotions, and deeds, shouldn't we hold those relationships to a higher standard?

On more than one occasion, I have had to distance myself from a friend, due primarily to the fact that they were adversely impacting my emotions. Quite frequently, I separate myself and even slow down the development of friendships because of that very thing—especially when it comes to developing relationships with coworkers.

While teaching is a tremendous profession, not all teachers feel that way. Some focus on conversations that are not edifying or uplifting. Far too often, many teachers just want to gripe about their students. This is not a healthy emotional environment to be in, especially for me since I want to have as much positive impact on students as possible. In those circumstances, due to those tendencies, it stifles our growth as friends. Life is too short to focus on the negative all the time.

Leadership expert John Maxwell is a *New York Times* best-selling author, speaker, and leadership trainer. In his book, *Sometimes You Win—Sometimes You Learn*, Maxwell writes: "If you want to be someone who embraces positive change, you need to hang around with positive learners [2]." That statement echoes my sentiment that taking a true pulse of our friendships can help us preserve our emotional state.

Self-Talk

Do you get really angry at yourself when you make a mistake? Maybe call yourself an idiot or something worse? Hands down, the most important and influential voice in a person's life is their own. Speaker, trainer, and business consultant Al Walker profoundly sums up the power of our inner voice with his comment: "The most important words we'll ever utter are those words we say to ourselves, about ourselves, when we're by ourselves [3]."

Our inner voice can either defeat us before we start or boost us with the confidence to succeed. Only the individual knows what is being communicated by that self-talk. A tremendous gauge to measure your self-talk is to run your words through the filter of kind, uplifting, and truthful. If your self-talk is not kind, uplifting, or truthful, then there will be significant impact on your emotional state. I love the idea of writing down the words you speak to yourself. Sometimes visually seeing them can alter mental self-mutilation. Taking it a step further, can you imagine saying those same words to someone else, especially someone you love? According to the Mayo Clinic, positive self-talk can do the following:

◆ Increase life span.
◆ Lower rates of depression.

- ◆ Lower levels of distress.
- ◆ Provide greater resistance to the common cold.
- ◆ Improve psychological and physical well-being.
- ◆ Create better cardiovascular health and reduced risk of death from cardiovascular disease.
- ◆ Improve coping skills during hardships and times of stress [4].

On the contrary, negative self-talk can have the opposite effects, including damaging your health. In a student's world, negative self-talk can cause them to underperform on tests or in many other areas in their lives, so it is crucial for everyone to take an honest survey of how they talk to themselves.

Morning Routine

This is where the previously mentioned impactors of music, friends, and self-talk intersect. Repetition is a tool for learning, which is why I previously discussed morning routine. When trying to influence others to adapt their morning routine, it will take repetition of these ideas for the learner to internalize them.

According to market research company International Data Corporation, 80% of smartphone users check their phone within fifteen minutes of hopping out of bed. This can create a lasting daily impression on the user. If they gravitate towards checking social media responses on their favorite app, they might be inclined to receive that dopamine rush from each "like."

Envision with me someone rolling out of bed and grabbing their phone. Then, the dopamine rush begins from the "likes" they received overnight. Unfortunately, that may be a short-lived sensation. In just a split second, that dopamine can turn to the stress hormone cortisol, if they see someone else got more likes or they begin to compare themselves to others.

What is a common response? "Oh, forget it. I have to get ready anyway." Then they pop in their earbuds, put on some music, and step to the mirror to get ready for their day. All the while, the negative self-talk spawned by social media comparisons is brewing in their head.

Some possible remedies to starting your day off right, thus keeping your emotional health in balance, are starting your morning with:

◆ Meditation
◆ Listening to positive messages from podcasts or videos
◆ "Stacking" gratitude by remembering your blessings
◆ Prayer
◆ Leaving the phone untouched!

With just a few minor morning behavioral modifications, you can easily begin to better preserve your emotional success [5].

State

This has nothing to do with geographic location, whether that is Florida, Georgia, California, or somewhere in between. It has everything to do with understanding that your physical state can directly impact your emotional state. Hopefully, at some point in your life you have experienced how changing your motion has changed your mood. For example, you feel lethargic, so you go to the gym and leave the gym with more energy than when you arrived.

A Harvard University professor, Amy Cuddy, took this idea a step further by studying "power posing." Imagine standing like a superhero with your hands on your hips. The results of her 2012 study showed that when people engaged in power posing for just two minutes prior to a job interview, they were more likely to be hired. Six years later, after criticism from fellow social psychologists, Cuddy and her collaborators published a rebuttal, saying such posing was still a legitimate method to make yourself feel more powerful [6].

Using that information, picture how power posing could be used over vast areas of our lives—perhaps prior to an important presentation, widely-watched performance, or other event when a person needs confidence. This illustrates the power of understanding the relationship between our physical state and our emotional state.

Possessing an accurate gauge of your emotional state at all times is one of the best ways to maintain a healthy emotional state. The goal is to teach the learners how to recognize those things that can positively or negatively impact them. Armed with that awareness, they can manage their emotional influences and, thus, improve their emotional state.

Bowl Meeting: What Superlatives Are You?

Full transparency here: I am not a fan of superlatives because I think they focus on too many of the wrong things. With that being said, I was voted "Most Likely to Succeed" by my high school graduating class. That label haunted me for years, primarily because I felt like I never lived up to that distinction. Ironically, I definitely love asking my students this question.

I got this idea from a discussion with students in one of my classes. A handful of years ago, a yearbook teacher in my district printed a superlative in the yearbook that asked who was "most likely to go to jail." As you can guess, the teacher got into some trouble. The discussion in my class revolved around the idea of how interesting it would be to see how your classmates viewed your future: positive or negative. There was no way to ask that question without getting myself into some hot water, so I spun it for the students, asking them to pick the superlatives for themselves. This way they could reflect over how they view themselves AND how they think their peers view them. Here is how it unravels.

I ask the students the following: pick four superlatives—one that *you* think describes you. One you think your *teachers* would use to describe you. One you think your *parents* would use to describe you. One you think your *friends* would use to describe you. You cannot pick the same one for all four. Here is the list I share with my students to encourage them to think about how others might perceive them and how they perceive themselves.

1. Most likely to own their own business.
2. Most likely to create a new product.

3. Most likely to greatly impact others.
4. Most likely to be known for their giving heart.
5. Most likely to make friends with everyone.
6. Most likely to be a great parent.
7. Most likely to work a high-paying job.
8. Most likely to work with their hands.
9. Most likely to be unforgettable.
10. Most likely to be late.
11. Most likely to let down the team.
12. Most likely to procrastinate.
13. Most likely to live an unfulfilled life.
14. Most likely to stir the pot.
15. Most likely to let life pass them by due to laziness.
16. Most likely to miss out on opportunities because they lack passion.
17. Most likely to work a low-paying job.
18. Most likely to drop their phone in the toilet.

The first seven carry positive connotations, while eight and nine are more neutral. The remainder definitely carry a negative vibe. Having the students reflect on these questions created a unique discussion and an eye-opening experience for me.

Take for example, Lisa, Tammy, and Renee (names changed for the sake of this discussion). All three voted themselves "most likely to live an unfulfilled life." As you can imagine, red flags waved like crazy for me when I heard this. Each girl had a different reason for their response. Lisa went on to discuss how she is extremely fearful in life and how that fear is debilitating. Tammy emphasized how she just likes to stay home all the time. Renee shared her apprehension of trying anything new.

Another student, Edward, revealed how his opinion of himself was in stark contrast with how I or any of his other teachers viewed him. He labeled himself "most likely to miss out on opportunities because he lacks passion." However, he is a straight A student and has created some of the most creative designs for my class that I have ever seen. Christy's reflection shook me. She bluntly admitted she would one day work at a low-paying job and that her parents would agree, because of her lack of passion. What startled me was how she seemed entirely at peace with this.

Even considering all those revelations and more, what deeply resonated with me were these next two examples. Mark stated his teachers would vote him "most likely to create a new product." When asked why, he mentioned a project he completed two years earlier, where he had to create something. His teacher at the time praised him and said she could see him being on the network TV show, *Shark Tank*. Remember, she had said this to him *two years* before. Yet, he has carried that comment with him to this day. Wow! The power of one positive comment. Then Justin shared how his teachers would vote him "most likely to miss out on opportunities because he lacks passion." His example came from a piano teacher, also expressed two years earlier. The instructor told him he was talented but lacked passion playing the piano.

I share both examples because of how what would seem like two harmless comments can live on—in fame or infamy. It struck a chord with me, making me recognize how impactful what we say to our learners can be. I hope these examples help you see how such discussions can lead to deeper discussion with each student. The overall activity gives you a snapshot of their psyches and challenges the learners to perform a self-evaluation. It also allows you to easily transition into the next Bowl Meeting. Now the learners have a solid grasp of who they are, it is time to really dive into who they want to be. The next chapter is a catalyst to doing just that.

✅ Key Takeaways

1. In order for anyone to be truly successful, they must be emotionally healthy.
2. Their choice in music and in friends can severely impact a student's emotional well-being.
3. How students communicate (self-talk) to themselves has a strong influence on one's emotional state.
4. Start the morning off with motivation!

🗨 Points to Ponder—Chapter 8

1. What aspect of your morning routine drains your emotional state?
2. Are there ways you address your students that leave a lasting impression on them, either good or bad?

References

1. Snahram Heshmat, "Music, Emotion, and Well-being: How Does Music Affect the Way We Think, Feel, and Behave?", *Psychology Today*, August 25, 2019, https://www.psychologytoday.com/us/blog/science-choice/201908/music-emotion-and-well-being
2. C. John *Maxwell, Sometimes You Win—Sometimes You Learn: Life's Greatest Lessons Are Gained from Our Losses* (New York: Center Street, 2013), 191.
3. "Al Walker Quotes," *GoodReads*, https://www.goodreads.com/quotes/113472-the-most-important-words-we-ll-ever-utter-are-those-words, accessed August 10, 2021.
4. Mayo Clinic Staff, "Positive thinking: Stop negative self-talk to reduce stress," https://www.mayoclinic.org/healthy-lifestyle/stress-management/in-depth/positive-thinking/art-20043950, accessed August 10, 2021.
5. Chloe Tejada, "Why Your Phone Shouldn't Be A Part Of Your Morning Routine," *HuffPost Canada*, December 12, 2019, https://www.huffingtonpost.ca/entry/dont-check-phone-in-morning_ca_5df24c1ae4b01e0f295b6d0a
6. Kim Elsesser, "Power Posing Is Back: Amy Cuddy Successfully Refutes Criticism," *Forbes*, April 3, 2018, https://www.forbes.com/sites/kimelsesser/2018/04/03/power-posing-is-back-amy-cuddy-successfully-refutes-criticism/?sh=3a6a449c3b8e

9

Attainable Goals

Handing Students the Tools for Setting Realistic Dreams

Once the students have a good handle on self-reflection, I shift to this question during a class:

Bowl Meeting: What Is a Goal You Can Obtain in the Next Three Months?

Up to this point, I have spent a ton of time challenging learners to discover who they are and who they want to be. This Bowl Meeting is where they must put words into actions. Understanding yourself is the precursor to setting goals and putting together a life map.

There is plenty of information disseminated out there on learning the importance of goal setting. However, I challenge you to show me one successful person (I know that definition is relative) who didn't set a goal on their road to success. People do not fall into success. They plan for it and work hard to achieve it. With that said, teaching your learners the right questions will give them a foundation to start setting goals in their lives.

DOI: 10.4324/9781003374497-9

> "If you fail to plan, you plan to fail."
> —That guy on a $100 bill

Good ol' Ben Franklin was more than implying that without well-thought-out goals we are setting out on a body of water without a sail. Goal setting provides several benefits that I will touch on briefly.

- Establishing a goal provides for greater focus. As learners progress down their journey, having a goal in mind can keep them on target.
- Likewise, setting goals can keep them motivated and help fight procrastination. Once a learner sets a goal and has discussed that goal, others can provide some gentle peer pressure by asking about it. This will increase a student's desire to perform because there is social accountability.
- Goal setting provides a sense of achievement. The learners must keep in mind what they will gain from setting and accomplishing their goals. This mindset will propel the learner forward with a greater tenacity than if they only focus on what they are having to give up.

Working SMARTER, Not Harder

There is a great acronym used to describe how to set goals—setting SMARTER goals. The original SMART phrase goes back to 1981 and George Moran, a consultant and former director of corporate planning for Washington Water Power Company, who published a paper about a way for reaching management's goals and objectives [1]. You can use this as your foundation when teaching your learners about goals.

S: Specific
The more specific a learner is with the goal, the more likelihood of success. It does little to say, "I want to get a good job." What

specifically does that mean? "Good" is a relative term. Is that in a certain industry, earning a certain amount of money? Similarly, if a person sets out to lose weight, he needs to set the goal of a specific number of pounds, not just "to lose weight." Specifics provide a clear goal, but also allow the learner to know when they have reached that goal. It is also important to keep in mind not just what is lost, but what is gained. Perhaps a person's weight-loss goal is at its heart a way to build self-esteem, which leads to the "M."

M: Meaningful

A goal must be meaningful to the creator to provide the motivation to accomplish it. This provides the "why" behind the goal. For a student, it could look like, "I will prepare for the SAT three nights a week for forty-five minutes per session so I can score a 1250 and earn a scholarship." This student's goal is clear, but the meaning behind achieving the goal is free tuition. That is a strong motivator! This could provide added freedom to this student's family, so they are not saddled with high college expenses.

A: Achievable

You could interpret this as meaning a realistic goal as well. I don't want to rain on anyone's parade, but some goals are not achievable. For example, a person might have certain physical limitations that hinder them from achieving that goal (seen any five-foot-tall folks dunking a basketball lately?). Remember the earlier discussion on passions versus gifts? This is why the goals have to be within the reach of the creator. A learner shouldn't say they are going to work hard and in two weeks boost their GPA from a 1.5 to a 4.0. That is not realistic.

Before you start beating me up about limiting goals and dreams, I am quite aware of individuals who have overcome adversity and odds to achieve mighty goals. For example, Shaquem Griffin, who played football at the University of Central Florida. Griffin has only one hand, yet he ran the forty-yard dash at the NFL Combine in 2018 in 4.38 seconds, the fastest time for a linebacker in fifteen years. Despite his handicap, he was drafted that spring by Seattle Seahawks and three years later signed a one-year contract with the Miami Dolphins. Griffin has accomplished goals that are amazing for a person with both hands, let alone just one. Keep in mind it also shows he has a gift that is coupled with his passion; he worked diligently to increase his talent.

Still, setting achievable goals is important for building momentum. By accomplishing a smaller, short-term achievable goal, a student will start the ball rolling to achieving much grander long-term goals. This in turn builds self-confidence and motivation.

R: Relevant

If a goal is not relevant to the student or person creating it, then why work to accomplish it? If a student's goal is to learn Mandarin to help them become an international business lawyer, then that is relevant. However, if they wish to become a school-teacher in the US, the goal to learn Mandarin would need to have some other anchoring purpose. The goal needs to be relevant to a person's ultimate outcome.

T: Time-Bound

Many goals fail because they are not associated with a specific time boundary. Take the previous example about learning Mandarin. Each step of the way there should be set time boundaries and small interim goals to accomplish such a large undertaking. For example: "I will complete Mandarin lessons 1-5 on the Rosetta Stone software by August 15th."

Adding time constraints creates a need for urgency but also the opportunity to celebrate the accomplishment. Students are groomed from five years old on that when they reach a certain milestone, such as the end of the school year, it is time to celebrate and enjoy it. They are rewarded with time off. As adults, we still need that time constraint and goals to strive for. Thus, the crucial nature of time-bound goals. Think of how many more weight loss plans succeed when the individual has a specific time frame in mind, such as an upcoming wedding or a high school reunion. We are hardwired to have solid time boundaries. Let's use them to our advantage and obtain our goal.

E: Evaluate

The engineering design process is iterative, meaning the person constantly cycles back through the process to make improvements to their product. Goal setting is the same way—they need to be continually evaluated. A student or other learner should write down their goals in order to refer to them at any time and continually make adjustments or check their progress toward obtaining the goal. Far too many New Year's resolutions have failed because the person doesn't revisit and evaluate them throughout the year. Evaluating goals with regularity means they become part of a person's psyche, which then leads to greater success.

R: Readjust

The last step in creating a SMARTER goal is be prepared to readjust your approach or the method you are using to obtain that success. Once you have evaluated the effectiveness of your goal, you then will need to make the necessary adjustments to obtain it. If a student's goal is to learn Mandarin, and Rosetta Stone is not helping as expected, maybe they need to consider a tutor or some other form of learning. Readjusting the goal can ensure the goal setter reaches the final destination. In addition, readjusting a goal can bring new life into a goal that might have run out of steam [2].

Contributing to Success

To return to the facets of success chart I discussed previously and which is shown again here as Figure 9.1, once a student understands how to write a SMARTER goal, it is important to emphasize how they should set goals in all areas of their lives. This will contribute to their definition of success. A great analogy I once heard involves viewing this chart like a wheel. If any of those areas are low, then how will that wheel perform? Bumpy and wobbly at best, which makes for a rough ride! When teaching goal setting, it is imperative to make this connection between the learners' definitions of success, and goal setting.

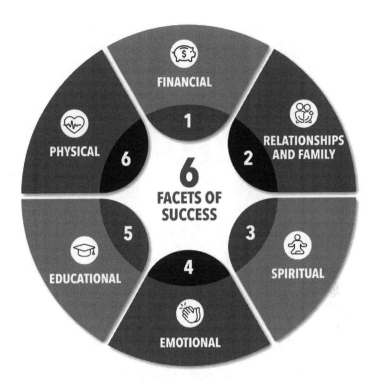

FIGURE 9.1 Here again is a visual representation of the facets of success.

To connect goal setting back to the lesson on defining success, as learners continue to update their "Facets of Success" chart, they are essentially setting goals for themselves. This is a fantastic practice. However, they need to see that life's big goals are essentially comprised of small goals (or stepping stones) to get there. If they just "talk" about these goals, then it might feel great on the surface to have set goals, but it will ultimately lead to regrets when they don't accomplish them. They have to thoroughly map out all the small accomplishments that need to happen along the way to reach their ultimate goal. The chart acts as their "map."

Angela Duckworth—whom I mentioned in Chapter 4—in *Grit: The Power of Passion and Perseverance* describes this as having goal hierarchy [3]. This is easiest understood through an example of a student, Melissa, who wants to go to college. She needs to be able to visualize and plan out what that looks like. This next example in Figure 9.2 is a simplistic version of what it could look like if she wants to get a Bright Futures scholarship, one offered by the state of Florida.

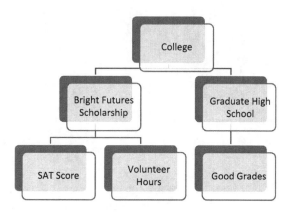

FIGURE 9.2 Visual example of how a student can plan out their steps to college.

Even with this example, each of the beginning subcategories could (and should) be broken into smaller categories and goals. For example, achieving an adequate SAT score could mean setting goals to take test preparatory courses and then studying thirty minutes a day for six weeks prior to the test. Volunteer hours could be broken up into a certain amount achieved per week, month, and year leading up to graduation. The good grades subcategory has a ton of areas that it could be broken into, such as grade level and subject area. This is just one example of a hierarchy of goals. Each of the facets of success listed previously should contain such planning.

Assembly Line Thinking

One thing that troubles me so much about education is its "assembly line" aspects. Today's framework for schools has its roots in the Industrial Revolution. Education is formatted to create more cogs in the wheels of progress. From kindergarten through twelfth grade, students are expected to remain focused and work toward success. Yet, we never teach them how because they are confined by the framework of the established education system.

Then at age eighteen, we turn them loose to make what typically is the second most expensive decision they will make in life (where to go to college). What information have we provided them to make a sound decision? How well have we guided them in the decision-making process? Defining their passions, success, motivation, and learning how to set goals is more than a push in the right direction—it is a rocket launch. If you are still not convinced why we should teach these topics, check out these statistics.

I gathered the following information from three sources: the US Department of Education, College Board, and the National Center for Education Statistics. I share it with you so you can understand the cost of NOT teaching your students about goal setting or how to ask the right questions.

1. Within three years of initial enrollment, about 30% of undergraduates who declared a major had changed their major at least once.
2. About half (52%) of students who originally declared math as a major switched within three years. Math majors change majors at a rate higher than that of students in all other fields, both STEM and non-STEM, except the natural sciences.
3. About one in ten students change majors more than once [4].
4. $37,650: The average annual cost for tuition and fees at a private university in 2021 [5].
5. $10,560: The average annual cost for tuition and fees at a public university in 2021 [5].
6. Nearly 60% of students who enter college will not graduate within six years [6].

That is a lot of time and money at risk for a student to walk into college and say, "I think I want to major in _____." Don't we owe it to our students (and their wallets) to at least start the discussion and planning process now? Learning these lessons does not ensure they will not switch majors, but by taking a proactive stance and giving them ample time to reflect, plan, and set goals, they can make much more informed decisions.

The previous statistics only address the importance of learners planning out their education and career. As many of us have experienced, not planning or setting goals in other facets of life can have much longer lasting financial and emotional impacts. This is why everyone should set goals in all facets of success. The benefits of goal setting far outweigh the disadvantages. Besides, learning early in life to set goals and achieve those goals builds confidence and self-esteem.

> "Self-confidence is not something you are born with; it is something you build."
>
> —Author unknown

Consider having your learners write down goals for the coming week, coming month, next six months, next year, and the next five years. Revisit them periodically to evaluate their progress. These can be the tiers used in their success chart. Starting off, make sure some of the goals are small, yet attainable. This starts the ball rolling and gains momentum. Then if you have the gumption, celebrate those goals. My next example will show you how.

Whoa, Where Did That Come From?

Have you ever walked by something dozens of times and not actually noticed it? Then one day, wham! You finally SEE it. This was the case with me. Day after day, I walked past a coworker's wall display about goals, and never once did I actually notice it. Not until my mindset switched to thinking about goals did it register how great it was.

Our brains often operate this way, due in part to something called the "Reticular Activating System" (RAS). Since our brains are bombarded with tons of information all the time, the RAS acts like a filter system, allowing in only what it deems important. A good example is buying a car—let's say a Jeep Cherokee. The moment you roll out with your Cherokee, you start seeing them everywhere. Why? Your RAS allows that information through since you are focused on your new car and consider this "important" information.

When you start focusing on something, then your RAS will siphon information pertinent to your focus and transmit it to your conscious mind. It acts like a big, red blinking sign saying, "Look here!" This will give you more "proof" or support for what you believe, whether positive or negative. The whole-time evidence to the contrary could literally be right in front of you, but your RAS filters it out. This is why it is important for learners to focus on the positive aspects of fulfilling their goal, not the negative. Their RAS will feed them what they focus on, whether positive or negative. Think of it as a magnifying glass through which they see the world.

Back to this fantastic project of my coworker. He starts the year by having students write their goals on an outline of their shoe. He then posts it on his wall. Envision a wall with dozens and dozens of cut out footprints on it. It is a very visual representation of their goals. As the year progresses and they accomplish their described goal, they get to take it down and add another one to the wall. By the end of the year, they have a stockpile of "feet" to take home, representing the goals they have accomplished. Some of the students share pretty revealing goals like one I saw stating, "Don't be sad." This also provided the teacher with a snapshot of his students' psyche. I love this example and to think, I would have never "seen" it if my focus hadn't shifted, and my RAS deemed it important.

Just as setting and meeting goals can create momentum, blowing them off creates a tolerance for mediocrity and creates a momentum in the wrong direction. This can be a slippery slope for learners that ferments in their minds a new option; an option without challenges, and an option that initially might be easier. The difficulty with goal setting is there is no way to measure the goals *not obtained*. There is no way of measuring the dreams *not accomplished*. There are great dangers in building a tolerance for ignoring or blowing off goals because it leads to those facets of success being unfulfilled.

If we dedicate some time and focus to teaching others about goal setting, then it will break through their RAS filter, allowing them to *see* ways they can accomplish their goals and deem goal setting as something worth "seeing." Essentially, this is what I am trying to do to your RAS: reprogram it to realize that teaching others these lessons is important. That way, you will devote some of your focus to it and share these ideas with your learners.

Aiming Higher

In my classroom, after the Bowl Meeting where I ask them to think about a goal they can accomplish in the next three months, I challenge them to plan out how to accomplish it. In Figure 9.3, you will see an example of student planning in regard to SMARTER goals (the template for this appears in the Appendix C). This begins the process of students internalizing the value of goal setting, and forces them to think about all the intricate steps that need to be taken to accomplish their goals.

Those intricate steps in obtaining a goal can be outlined in a daily "to-do" list. Therefore, after having the students develop a three-month goal, I encourage you to have each learner create a to-do list for each day. Then, as they complete those written tasks, they have a daily sense of accomplishment. Maybe it is because I am old school, but I think writing it down and physically crossing it off is way better than having a digital list.

Also, according to one study conducted by a psychology professor in California, by writing down your goals, you are 42% more likely to obtain them.[7] At the time I started working on this book, the world was battling the early stages of the coronavirus pandemic. One weekly assignment I had my students complete during that time of "distance learning" was submitting to me a copy of their daily to-do list. The road to success is paved with discipline, and discipline is accomplished by established routines.

This is why it is so important for students to develop routines and even track them. It begins with the small routine of establishing a checklist. Then, that concept can grow into establishing one-week, one-month, one-year, five-year, and ten-year goals. As part of their daily to-do list, they can devote time to working on their three-month goal. As they progress through

	Questions to ponder	Responses
Specific	What exactly do you want to accomplish?	I want to reach the next rank in Boy Scouts.
Measurable	How will you know when you have completed your goal? How will you measure your progress?	I will have the Second Class rank.
Achievable	What knowledge do you need to ensure success?	I will need to know the requirement to get the rank (Add a list of those requirements)
Relevant	Why is this important to you?	Because being a high ranking Scout can open job opportunities.
Time Bound	When will you complete this goal?	Hopefully by the next court of Honor (when is that?)
Evaluate	When will you check in on your progress? How are you progressing?	At every troop meeting, campout and Scouting event, I can check on my progress and get more things done.
Re-adjust	What might you need to alter to accomplish this goal?	I need to alter my routine to incorporate scouts.

FIGURE 9.3 Student example of setting SMARTER goals.

each daily established to-do list, they are picking up momentum. With momentum comes change and the reward of accomplishing bigger life goals.

It's All About You

You didn't think I would write a book about personal reflection without challenging you to do a little, did you? The next couple pages can drastically shape your classroom. This portion is going to be interactive, so I need you to hop right in and grab a writing utensil and some paper. If you are not a teacher, the following information still has value for you. You will just need to switch out the following:

1. Employees for students.
2. Office for classroom.
3. Fiscal year for school year.

---

1. In one sentence, what is the ONE message you want your students to understand by the end of the school year?
2. In one sentence, describe your classroom (not the physical layout).
3. When leaving your classroom at the end of the year, what do you want students to
   a. ... know?
   b. ... feel?
   c. ... say?
4. What value are you bringing to your students?
5. What NEW value do you bring to your classroom today?

Each of these questions merits a closer look.

1. In one sentence, what is the ONE message you want your students to understand by the end of the school year?

   This question gets you to frame your goal for the entire year. It might change during the 180 days, but it should only be slightly modified. My answer to that first question is: "With the right attitude, consistency in planning goals, and the ability to problem-solve, I can achieve MY definition of success beyond my wildest imagination." Every day you should reflect on your answer to that question and evaluate if you are on track, or if you need to adjust your heading.

2. In one sentence, describe your classroom.

   Realizing this is a broad and ambiguous question gets you to contemplate how you visualize your classroom. Is it fun? Loud? Peaceful? Teacher-driven? Dictator-driven? Do you facilitate or delegate? Would your students agree with your perception? I answer this question this way: My classroom is a training ground for an army of problem-solvers.

What does that look like? When you come to my classroom, rarely will you see me giving a lecture. The students are interacting, building, making a mess, and then redesigning. First, you accurately describe your classroom, then once again, constantly reevaluate if you are maintaining this description. If it is not how you envision your class to be, then change it!

3. When leaving your classroom at the end of the year, what do you want your students to ... know ... feel ... say?

This is such an important question. It really is the thermometer of your classroom. Yes, they need to know your subject area, but what do you *really* want them to know? This one should reflect the answer to the first question (plus, maybe a few other things). What do you want them to feel? Truly, how do you want them to feel walking out your door: inspired, invigorated, depressed, aggravated, or motivated? It is up to you. For me, I want them to feel empowered to take on any tsunami life produces.

Lastly, what do you want them to say? "Mr. Motivation inspired me to be an author?" or, "Mrs. Great Teacher redirected my whole attitude?" I want them to say, "Mr. Yuhasz empowered me to think deeper, love broader, and fail my way to success." By constantly revisiting this question, you can get a temperature gauge of your classroom. Are they leaving your classroom each day knowing, feeling, and saying those things?

4. What value are you bringing to your students?

Easy question, right? This might be the lengthiest answer yet, and that is great! If you make sure to look back over the answer to this question throughout the school year, it will be a gentle reminder of what you are trying to accomplish. The value I bring to my students are the questions discussed in this book.

Although this was mentioned before, it bears repeating. I also teach them about the exciting careers associated with the STEM fields. This is what motivates me to have the bomb squad come and show off their cool robots or have engineers from NASA or Lockheed come chat up my students or take my students to check out the assembly line at a Frito Lay manufacturing plant. This is the value I bring to my students. I bet you must have some great things on your list as well.

5. What NEW value do you bring to your classroom today?

    This might come across as me throwing down the gauntlet, but that is not the case. We cannot be in the business of promoting "learning" if we are unwilling to learn. This is a challenge I extend to myself as well. What new concept, lesson, or idea are you bringing to these students? It is easy to get caught up in the same old lessons and teaching the same old curriculum. Well, how are you keeping your content fresh and inspired? It does not have to be a massive undertaking.

Almost daily, I search for something new to read in the field of aerospace. When I find something cool, like details on an upcoming SpaceX launch or newly released plans for the United States to go back to the moon, I share it with my class. I literally show them the article and we discuss the exciting news. It does not have to be a massive undertaking, but I want to share with my students that learning doesn't ever stop. Every person should be dedicated to being a lifelong learner.

Creating Successful People

The five reflective questions I have just reviewed can better define your goals as a teacher or leader. Try sharing them with your students, learners, or employees while emphasizing how important their success is to you. The late Stephen Covey, author of *The 7 Habits of Highly Effective People*—which has sold more than twenty-five million copies—talked about how the reflective process reinforces the second habit of highly effective people: Begin with the end in mind [8]. If we always keep the end goal for our learners in mind, and even outlined in a "mission statement," we are more likely to achieve that end goal. Hopefully, that end goal is reminding your learners you are in the business of creating successful people. Figure 9.4 illustrates a student's perspective on the importance of this.

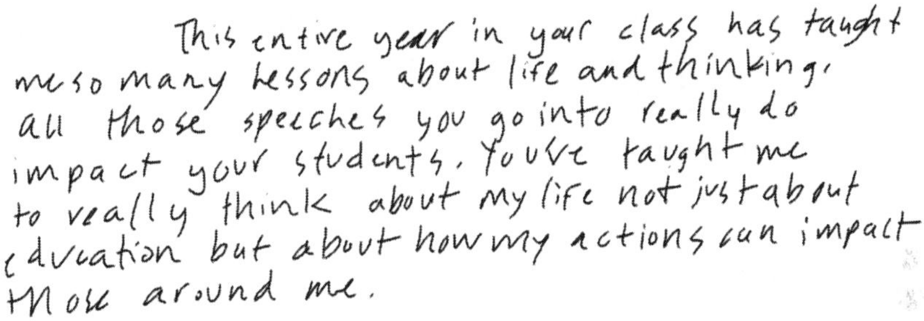

This entire year in your class has taught me so many lessons about life and thinking. All those speeches you go into really do impact your students. You've taught me to really think about my life not just about education but about how my actions can impact those around me.

FIGURE 9.4 A great student testimony of why it is important to teach these concepts.

When educating your students about goal setting, the following list should help you navigate the lesson.

1. Write down their initial goal.
2. Bounce that goal off the requirements of a SMARTER goal. Essentially, refine what they wrote.
3. Research who and what it will take to accomplish that goal. (Doesn't matter if it is a small or large goal.)
4. Predict roadblocks, hurdles, and challenges (emotional, social, financial).
5. Chunk it into small steps by doing daily "to-do" lists.
6. Celebrate the small victories along the way.
7. Continually evaluate progress. (Yes, this is part of a SMARTER goal, but it bears mentioning again.)

Before leaving the topic of goal setting, I want to circle back to a point I bulldozed over earlier: *It is crucial for goal setters to talk about their goals.* Goals should not be tucked away on a piece of paper between the cushions on the couch but placed on billboards. Discussing your goals with other people brings them into your circle. This means not only that they can help you along your journey, but it also promotes brainstorming and collaboration, and creates accountability. Share your goals with your learners. Lead by example.

If you do not accomplish your goal, talk to them about why that happened. If you did reach it, celebrate with them. Big or small, share your goals with your learners. It will encourage you to achieve it, and they will see you practicing what you preach. I have shared with my students my goals for this book and the progress I was making as I worked on it. We celebrated together! They are really great supporters. Begin sharing your goals with your class, coworkers, or others, so they can learn to share theirs with you. It really is a win/win scenario.

Through this brief description of the importance of goals and how to design a goal, I wish to challenge you to set goals for yourself, and not just your learners. If you are a teacher, those goals can revolve around classroom successes. However, think about how much more significant an impact you will make if you help people design goals that align with their success in life.

Before transitioning away from this discussion, I want to point out what everything thus far has been leading up to: The learners creating a clear-cut vision for their future. Time and time again, no matter who the successful person, they will share how they had a clearly defined vision of what they wanted to achieve. You will notice how I encouraged you and your learners throughout this chapter to set a vision. Creating a vision relates to defining success. Essentially, what you will have your individuals do is create a successful vision for the future. Then, setting goals helps that vision come to fruition and no longer remain just a dream. This leads me to the next chapter and the topic that can make or break success.

✓ Key Takeaways

1. Using the SMARTER acronym helps students to carve out setting attainable goals.

2. Establishing goals for your classroom aids in creating a successful learning environment.
3. It is crucial for goal setters to talk about their goals.

Points to Ponder—Chapter 9

1. Have you ever written down a goal and actually attained it?
2. How did that make you feel?
3. How can you structure this lesson to ensure you do periodic "goal checks" to help hold the students accountable?

References

1. Duncan Haughey, "A Brief History of SMART Goals," *Project Smart*, December 13, 2014, https://www.projectsmart.co.uk/brief-history-of-smart-goals.php. An article in *Inc.* magazine credits Doran, Arthur Miller, and James Cunningham for the idea, reportedly expressed in a 1981 article in *Management Review*. See "4 Ways to Make Your SMART Goals Even Smarter" by Wanda Thibodeaux, *Inc.*, December 18, 2019, https://www.inc.com/wanda-thibodeaux/4-ways-to-make-your-smart-goals-even-smarter.html

2. "Setting S.M.A.R.T.E.R. Goals: 7 Steps to Achieving Any Goal," *Wanderlust Worker*, https://www.wanderlustworker.com/setting-s-m-a-r-t-e-r-goals-7-steps-to-achieving-any-goal/, accessed August 11, 2021.

3. *Grit: The Power of Passion and Perseverance.*

4. The first three items in the college statistics came from "Beginning College Students Who Change Their Majors within 3 Years of Enrollment," *Data Point*, U.S. Department of Education, December 2017, https://nces.ed.gov/pubs2018/2018434.pdf

5. "How Much Does College Cost?" *CollegeData.com*, https://www.collegedata.com/resources/pay-your-way/whats-the-price-tag-for-a-college-education, accessed August 12, 2021.

6. "Fast Facts," *National Center for Education Statistics*, https://nces.ed.gov/fastfacts/display.asp?id=40, accessed August 12, 2021.

7. Marie Forleo, "Self-made Millionaire: The Simple Strategy That Helped Increase My Odds of Success by 42%," *CNBC*, September 13, 2019, https://www.cnbc.com/2019/09/13/self-made-millionaire-how-to-increase-your-odds-of-success-by-42-percent-marie-forleo.html

8. Originally published in 1989, Steven Covey's *The 7 Habits of Highly Effective People* was released in a twenty-fifth anniversary edition in 2013 by Simon & Schuster. In addition to the millions in print, as of mid-2021 the audio book had sold 1.5 million copies.

10

Directional Influences—Part I

Who Is Sculpting the Minds of Our Students?

As we continue this journey into thinking about thinking, I am reminded of a fifth grader I taught early in my career. Trisha presented daily challenges. She was the angriest student I have ever taught. Trapped in a dungeon of anger, she couldn't find a way out. She never did her math homework, a crucial tool for students at this age, and she snapped at other students incessantly. Instead of going toe to toe with her about her habits, one day I quietly pulled her outside and directed her to a blue bench.

Looking at her calmly, and with patience in my voice, I asked, "Why are you so angry ... all ... the ... time?" The rapidity of her response stunned me: "I am worried about my sister." She told me how the moment she arrived home, her mother's boyfriend would leave. Since her mom was already at work, this eleven-year-old student had to cook dinner for her little sister. No wonder she didn't care about adding mixed numbers—she was raising her sister!

After her explanation, tears flowed down her cheeks. What a cathartic release! It brought a breakthrough too. Her anger didn't vanish, but it waned. Somehow, she gained comfort out of communicating her situation to me. After this eye-opening exchange,

DOI: 10.4324/9781003374497-10

I realized, there are many layers to a student and their perceptions of education, even at a young age. Plus, their attitude is rooted in events and circumstances beyond our control.

It dawned on me that attitude is by far the most influential thing that allows a person to find success and fulfillment. Altering one's attitude is not easy, but it can be done. What proceeds are recollections of how I have altered my attitude and influenced students' attitudes. The tools I share can truly reshape a person's life. In order to accomplish such a lofty goal, we must first look at three "attitude influencers" on our students or learners: ours, their social network, and their parents. There are many others, but I will focus on these three. The truth is we are quite limited. We can only change our attitude, influence our learners' attitudes, and accept their parents' attitudes. You will notice in Figure 10.1 how each of those influences interact and can impact our students.

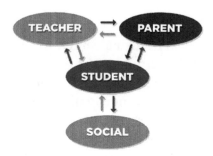

FIGURE 10.1 The flow of student influences.

Where'd You Get That Attitude?

In this chapter and the next, I will take an in-depth look at examples of the following directional influences:

1. Teacher/student
2. Teacher/parent/student
3. Parent/student
4. Parent/teacher
5. Student/social
6. Student/student

A word of caution before you start reviewing these individually: this discussion grew so lengthy that I had to break it into two chapters. I review the first three in this chapter and the last three in Chapter 11.

It is imperative that you understand how these all weave together. In the following examples, it will be challenging at times to distinguish whose attitude is influencing whom, due to their tightly knit character. Each of these interactions represent a two-way street. As you are aware, a student's attitude can positively or negatively influence us, and vice versa. Once you introduce a parent's attitude into the mix, it can prove quite challenging, or rewarding. Understanding and analyzing the relationships of these three influences is what will open the door to influencing your student.

Teacher/Student

The first point of focus will be on the teacher/student portion of the diagram. We are going to examine not only how the attitude of the teacher can influence the student, but how the attitude of the student can impact the teacher. Immersing ourselves in the first, if someone who is not a teacher overheard you talking about your career, would it inspire that person to walk away and say, "Wow! Being a teacher must be great!"? Or would they say, "Teaching must be a miserable career!"? Success begins with the leader and can be a direct reflection of the leader's attitude. If you struggle with your personal attitude toward your job, your students will pick up on this. Teaching students to have the right attitude starts with their fearless leader. There will always be challenges in the workplace. But, overall, if you are unhappy in your classroom, your students will be too.

> *Besides, a good attitude opens up opportunities!*

Currently, I am a STEM teacher—and I love my job! However, this would not be the case today if I had not changed my dismal attitude a few years ago. A person at the district level approached the science team at my school, offering one of us an opportunity to teach a curriculum called Project Lead the Way. It involved a host of unpaid training courses AND we had to pass a test to add something to our teaching certificate. Since this would cost three hundred dollars out of our own pockets, none of us were initially too excited about it. Thankfully, I decided to jump on the grenade and make it happen. It was the best decision I have made in my professional career; it has completely reshaped what I teach. The scary part is it almost didn't happen. A sour attitude nearly kept me from this great option. Conversely, a good attitude can carry you a long way and create opportunities for great student impact—as in this next example.

The last few days of a school year are always so fun for me. I truly love the freedom afforded teachers. We can teach students about anything without the confining shackles of a test looming over everyone's heads. (Full disclosure here: most teachers do not feel that way. They view it as drudgery and just show their students a movie.) One year, my principal asked me to share something with the faculty to keep them inspired to finish the year strong.

I jumped into action and formulated a five-minute lesson on the Reticular Activating System (RAS) to the faculty. After explaining RAS, I encouraged them to take the last three days to teach their students some of the right questions and four careers associated with their subject area. After my short speech, the first comment expressed by a coworker was, "That was a long-winded way to tell us to keep focused the last three days." Laughing, I replied, "You are right." (Clearly, the message was not well received by that person.)

At the end of the day though, the "paycheck" arrived in the mail. A long-term substitute teacher in language arts wrote a note saying, "Hey, thanks for that message earlier. I went back and researched and taught my students four careers they can get in language arts." Perfect! That meant more than 150 students would be positively impacted. She had the right attitude and her students just learned about the options they have at their fingertips.

The Award Goes to … Educators!

Now, it doesn't feel that way sometimes, even though teachers have to be the best actors and actresses in the world. We must constantly don a happy face when we get a transfer student in our class who already has a bad reputation. When our administration requires us to implement the "newest" trend in teaching, we must imagine it is absolutely great. We also must support it when our administration requires it to be implemented. We must put on our Denzel Washington or Sandra Bullock act as if we are dying to hear about a student's weekend, right after we received an email from a parent blaming us because her daughter is missing work and has a low grade. Seriously, we can act!

At times, a theatrical, positive attitude can go a long way. One class I teach requires students to take an industry certification exam for some CAD (computer aided design) software. Every year I have taught this course, the "powers-that-be" change the test. So, every year, I do not know the format of the test. The second year administering it, I finally got to preview the newest version. In looking over the exam format, the number of questions, and time restraints, I was extremely frustrated about having to give my students this exam. I considered it an overly tough test and poorly designed. In addition, I felt the way they had to toggle between the computer-based exam and the software was ludicrous.

Venting to someone at the district level, I said to him, "I am hoping just 25% pass." Now, you better believe my students saw a different side of that coin. I cheered them on, encouraged them, and told them: "100% of you will pass." Wouldn't you know it, 100% did! When I saw the results, I bounced off the walls with excitement. Grabbing a kid's skateboard, I zoomed up and down the halls yelling, "100%, baby!"

When we celebrated after the success in the classroom, I was transparent with the students, though, confessing, "I was worried. I really only expected 25% of you to pass." One student didn't hesitate, responding, "But you told us we were all going to pass." After eating my humble pie, I learned a valuable lesson:

> *Present a good attitude to students, even when you don't have one. They might believe your acting skills ... "I'd like to thank the academy ..."*

Think back to the discussion of the RAS. Once programmed, RAS will put out big red flags so you recognize all the negative data that supports your viewpoint. That viewpoint could be a negative one toward a test, like I just mentioned. First and foremost, it takes a recognition of the negative attitude. Then, it takes the strong desire to make that change. At times, this can be a weekly, daily, or even hourly effort, but it can be done. It all depends on how deeply anchored is the negative attitude.

I shared with you how in the past, I achieved a lot but never felt successful. Primarily because of my lousy, stinking, landfill-smelling, forsaken, porta-potty-on-a-hot-summer-day attitude. Don't get me wrong, I knew I needed an attitude adjustment; I was just unwilling to let go of those emotional anchors to the past so I could enjoy a positive future. It took constant reflection and evaluation, and then a willingness to let go of those anchors (which was the toughest part). My RAS was programmed to see all the negative things and ignore all the positive things that came from my lamentable past decisions.

A Tasmanian Angel

The exciting thing is your attitude can change. However, it will take some work. There are those rare moments, though, when an attitude can change with just a few words of positivity. Cue Mark B.

Mark was a student I learned to appreciate after I got over my fear of what he was going to bring to my classroom. Before the school year even started, I had six staff members from my school seek me out to talk about Mark. You'd better believe they were not coming to tell me about how great he was; in their eyes, he was the Tasmanian Devil. No joke, I was afraid to have this kid in my classroom before I even laid eyes on him. Still, left with no choice, I chose to be proactive and devise a plan. I couldn't treat him like his other teachers, nor could I let my fear of his inner rage paralyze me.

The first day of school I pulled him out of lunch, just so I could get some one-on-one time with him. We chatted and I learned more about him, including how much he loved football. My whole goal was to build a rapport with him so he could view me unlike any of his other teachers. This occurred several times over the next few weeks. To my surprise, it worked! I never once experienced a behavior problem with him.

This strategy paid off in future dividends. One Friday, on his way back to class after recess, Mark was burning with anger. He was ready to kill another student who had "wronged" him on the football field. I physically stood in front of him so he could not aggressively go after the other student, saying, "Your life is going to have plenty of Jeffries in it. If you don't learn to manage your anger and attitude, you are going to spend your whole life fighting. Even if you win the fight, you will lose. This will ruin your plans to play football."I let him sit outside for a while to cool down. He never attacked that other student. I successfully planted the idea in his mind that he had to make a proactive choice not to let another student/player have that much of a negative impact on him.

Years later, I had the privilege of running into Mark. He told me how he vividly remembered that day and thanked me for that advice. The cool thing was how he brought up the conversation we had that day; I didn't ask him about it. He went on to describe how he had been following that advice ever since. I am still amazed at how much an impact teachers can have on students with just a few words. The example of Mark is one example of how a teacher can positively influence a student's attitude. Truthfully, I have not always handled challenging situations well. As evident in the diagram, students can impact us, and not always in a positive fashion.

Ankle Trackers and Parole Officers

Be honest: have you ever taken it personally when students don't do their work? Don't lie here. You're amongst friends. Of course, you have; we all have. It wasn't until my tenth year of teaching that I began the slow process of changing my attitude toward their decisions to not perform. Let me tell you, that was a tough year of teaching. I transitioned from teaching elementary school to middle school. Wow, did I have so much to learn! I was stepping into a situation where, unbeknownst to me, my classroom was going to have students with ankle trackers, babies, and parole officers (they left that part out during my interview). With those students, I could track back and quickly determine the source of their challenging attitudes.

It was the things you would predict with underperforming students, like lack of support at home, no real mentorship, and no value associated with education. There was one kid, though, whom I could just not wrap my head around. I am going to call him Chachi. He was one of the few students who came from a lower-middle-class home. There was no evidence of neglect or need on his part. He wore decent clothing, had plenty of school supplies, and a love of skateboarding. He wasn't disrespectful or belligerent. He was very bright, but he just did not do a THING! When I say he didn't do a thing, I mean he did not even bother to take out a pencil.

Nothing motivated Chachi. Calls home. Threats of detention. Extra homework. Nothing. Nice to him. Nothing. Mean to him. Nothing. Nothing. Nothing. Nothing. Up to this point in my career, I could always get a student to do some work. (Even my student who had a parole officer because she slashed another student in the face.) But not Chachi. This master of nothingness triggered a putrid wound inside me. This was now personal!

It got to the point where we started butting heads in class. Let me rephrase that; I was butting heads with him. I just couldn't accept the fact that he would not work for me. I would lose sleep over it. Naturally, he was in my first-period class, so I would spend my day steaming about it. I gave this student too much power over my attitude. Something had to change (and, of course, it had to be me).

> *You can't control your students. You can only control your attitude towards them, even though this is not an easy lesson to learn.*

Thankfully, before the end of the school year, I experienced a breakthrough, which gave me peace with Chachi. The breakthrough occurred when I truly understood—and embraced the fact—that I cannot control my students in any way, shape, form, or fashion. So, no more did I bash my head against his. On the extremely rare occurrence of him doing something, my goodness, did I make a big deal about it: "Ladies and gentlemen, I must warn you. The end of time is near. Chachi did some work!"

The kids would laugh. Chachi would laugh. (He really had a great personality.) We would celebrate, but the next day he would be back to doing nothing. I can't tell you how many times I have had to learn the lesson about controlling my attitude. It really is a lifelong challenge to constantly regulate it. But, with a lot of practice and a growth mindset, it can happen. If students can learn how to do this early in life, what an amazing life awaits them.

Parent/Student

The parent/student influence has an enormous impact on a student's attitude as well. In the ideal world, parents and teachers will share the ultimate goal regarding our students' attitudes, which is to make them capable of weathering whatever storms come their way. We certainly hope that our students will not have to undergo trials in life, but that is beyond our control. By teaching students earlier in life how to adjust their attitudes and to investigate what emotional or evidential reasons are behind why they think the way they do, we are putting them into a position of success.

> "Successful people are not people without problems. They are simply people who have learned to solve their problems."
> —Earl Nightingale [1]

I cannot talk about positive attitudes without talking about Connor, Riley, and Toby, three brothers who formed a band called Before You Exit. They live in Los Angeles now and have toured the world promoting some of their fantastic music. I had the privilege of teaching all three of them in fifth grade. Now, by no means am I taking credit for their great attitudes; their parents (Mark and Joan) started early on teaching them the power of a positive attitude, as well as modeling it. I reinforced that message in my classroom.

However, this attitude got put to the test on June 10, 2016. Before You Exit played playing a concert in their hometown of Orlando, Florida. They had a couple opening acts, including a singer named Christina Grimmie. Shortly after the concert ended, the venue still resounded with the sounds of screaming teenage fans and the chorus of the band's signature song, *Radiate*. Then, suddenly, it echoed with the sounds of gunshots. A crazed fan shot and killed Christina before turning the gun on himself.

At this point, the road to recovery and regaining a positive attitude was long and drawn out. They could have called it quits, if they had chosen to anchor their attitudes to that fateful night, but the three brothers were able to look back at their earlier lessons about attitude and began to do what they are so talented at … writing. From that horrific moment, they have produced the most heartfelt and amazing songs, including a tribute to Christina called *Clouds*.

I share this story with you to get you to see the importance of teaching learners the right questions. They might not have a great support system at home to help them navigate the kind of event Connor, Riley, and Toby had to endure. Most of our students do not enjoy such a strong support system. While we do not know what our students will face in this life, we can at least begin equipping them with the ways to better face what lies ahead.

The story of their father, Dr. Mark McDonough, is equally amazing and heart-wrenching. Now retired, Dr. McDonough was an accomplished plastic and reconstructive surgeon, but had every excuse to not amount to anything. When he was a teenager, his house caught fire. While searching for his mother through scorching heat and suffocating smoke, he suffered third degree burns over most of his body. Through this experience, he lost his mother, but never his spirit to survive despite enduring countless surgeries and skin grafts.

All the while, he developed an appreciation for the medical field, which led to his pursuit to make a difference and help those who suffered like he had. Do you think he passed on his desire and attitude to his sons? Without a doubt! Their mother, Joan, reinforced this positive ethos, since she is a pivotal cog in the wheel that turns this positive family. Dr. McDonough now can add published author to his resume, with his autobiography—*Forged Through Fire*—released by a major publisher in the fall of 2019.

Of course, even if students have supportive parents with good attitudes, it doesn't always mean they will recognize that. While discussing parents, I should reveal a little more about mine. As mentioned before, my father is an extremely hard-working man. His working two jobs for more than thirty years begs the question of "how?". Attitude. He is proud of what he does at both jobs and goes in each day with a good attitude. I never realized that until recently.

Coincidentally, my mother was my biggest fan. Growing up I played basketball six or seven days a week. No matter what, she always thought I was the best player on the court. She seemed to ignore that six-foot-six guy on the other team dunking all over us (and who went on to play pro football with the Los Angeles Raiders). Both my parents were selling good attitudes, but for many years, I sure wasn't buying them. I mention this point because it might take students hearing these things from someone else—namely you—before they internalize the power of attitude.

Teacher/Parent/Student

In a perfect world, all three parties would have optimistic outlooks on life, accompanied by positive attitudes. Unlike the examples listed above, many of our students do not have parents who convey positive attitudes. Therefore, as teachers, we need to set up a classroom environment that nurtures students and helps rewire such negativity. Parents can be one of the strongest conduits of poor attitudes. Without a doubt, you have witnessed poor attitudes coursing through parents, which are then discharged through their children (your learners). Time and time again, I have witnessed parents who place no importance on education and have utter disdain for authority. No wonder their child struggles in school with learning and poor behavior!

One example I witnessed of a parent teaching a child a negative attitude occurred while I was flying to Alabama. Picture this mother in her mid-thirties, huffing and puffing down the aisle with a four-year-old girl in tow. The mother is flailing her arms, sighing, mumbling, and grumbling. She finally arrives at her seat, which is in the row in front of me. The little girl hops on her seat, bursting with enthusiasm about her upcoming flying adventure. What does the mom say to her daughter? "Oh, this is so stressful, isn't it?" At this point, I had no idea what challenges they had faced getting to the airport, but I could tell her daughter had no sense of anything being stressful.

In the above circumstance, the mother met her conditions with a negative attitude and decided to cast her feelings on her daughter. Again, it may have been thoroughly stressful for her, but did that have to be communicated to the little girl? No doubt, situations like this occur a lot with our learners. We need to anticipate students being raised under such circumstances. We can teach them to be proactive and cut off negative attitudes and feelings prior to letting them rankle and develop. This can alter the behaviors and they, the students, can decide if they are going to allow their conditions to define them.

Okay, Who Brought the Sunscreen?

Sometimes we need a little extra SPF to block out the negative "light." To give you an example directly from my classroom, a student I'll call Sylvia had a quite challenging attitude. In addition to being quick to complain, when an assignment was due, she typically turned it in late. Repeatedly, she dealt out rapid excuses while swiftly casting blame on others. No doubt, you have taught this type of student before or been around someone like this.

My classes are heavily project-based group work. On the last project of the school year, Sylvia was running way behind. I always encourage students to come to my room anytime during the day to finish up their work, even if it is during lunch. Sylvia never capitalized on this offer. The night AFTER the project was due, Sylvia emailed me around 9:00 p.m. Her mother emailed me shortly thereafter, before I could even address Sylvia's note. Mother and daughter complained about Sylvia's partner and how unfair it had been to "stick" them together (Sylvia had had a whole week to get this done, good partner or not).

The next day in class, they had to present. Sylvia had little ready and did not meet the criteria of her engineering design challenge. Before you judge me, I always circulate and offer help or advice. Many students have perfected the art of looking busy. That doesn't bother me since it all comes out in the end during their presentations. After all the presentations, I emphasized with the class that sometimes in life you get dealt a good group to work with, or you get a lousy group. I reminded them it is their obligation to get their work done, regardless of the group to which they have been assigned.

Sylvia went home and told her mother what I said. Her mother didn't hesitate to complain about me via email, stating that no one should have to pull the weight of others. Had it been earlier in my career, this email would have bothered me. Thankfully, I have learned to avoid taking certain things personally. This parent did not understand all the circumstances, nor how little effort her child put into her work. I replied politely but directly, sharing with the mother the minimal effort put forth by her daughter and saying we could agree to disagree about the matter of working in groups.

I share this story to emphasize the challenge students have in overcoming poor parental attitudes. And, how easily a parent's attitude impacts their child, which in turn can impact the teacher. This example also connects back to the discussion of having a victim mentality. Sylvia is a product of her environment and clearly reflects the "light" the mother is radiating. This again is why we must be proactive in teaching students how to get and maintain a positive attitude.

> *Proactively anticipating challenging situations to curb the up rise of a negative attitude takes a continuous, conscious effort.*

While we are on the subject, being proactive is one way to cut short a bad attitude before it blossoms. If we can recognize the triggers that lead to a poor attitude in ourselves, we will have a strong likelihood of maintaining a positive attitude when they arrive. Think about when you go to the beach. If you watch the weather and plan accordingly, you know when to pack up and head home before you get caught in a storm. Your attitude is no different. Anticipate the rainy days and cherish the sunny ones, applying some sunscreen to block out that "negative" light.

Two Annoying Traits

The common saying is hope for the best, but plan for the worst. I think it is a bit more complicated than that, but essentially that is the gist of the matter. The important concept for your learners to grasp is to anticipate negative attitude triggers. You could center the discussion on this Bowl Meeting prompt:

Bowl Meeting: Name Two Personality Traits That Annoy You

Once they share their ideas, you can redirect the discussion back to how they can proactively anticipate those traits and healthily process them. Think back to the approach former student Mark took when he felt "wronged" on the football field. He absorbed this message of proactively anticipating negative attitude triggers and quickly applied it to his life. Mark is a great example of how students can learn how to recognize those triggers.

Still looking at the teacher/parent/student connection, it can also have an overwhelmingly positive impact. Abena is one of the most amazing parents I have had the honor of knowing;

I was fortunate enough to teach all three of her children. Despite the odds being stacked against this native of Ghana striving to raise three children as a single mother, she knew what it would take for them to succeed: hard work.

Yes, that meant putting in countless hours at a local grocery store to provide for her children's needs, but Abena knew that it also takes countless hours of supporting and nurturing her children so they can achieve success. Every time I saw her, she greeted me with a smile that would warm anyone's heart. Her children were the same way: positive, optimistic, and hardworking. Abena showed up at every school event, often still wearing her work uniform. This instilled in her children the value of education and how it relates to success. Her diligence paid off. All three children are academically successful: the youngest graduated as valedictorian of her class before heading to Harvard University.

Up to this point, I have moved gently through most of the diagram. Keep in mind that understanding all these connections can help you better impact your students. I have looked at how parents can positively and negatively impact a student. To start the next chapter, I will look more closely at an example of how the parent can impact the teacher.

✅ Key Takeaways

1. Students have numerous directional and attitudinal influences.
2. Educators impact student attitudes just as much as students impact educators' attitudes. Sometimes for the good; other times, for the worse.
3. By reflecting over negative personality traits, students can be redirected to see how they can proactively anticipate those traits and healthily process them.

💭 Points to Ponder—Chapter 10

1. Can you think of a time when parents got the best of you emotionally?

2. How could you have responded better?
3. Do you have a "breakthrough" student who no one else could reach but you?
4. Could you use the same techniques you used with them with others?

Reference

1. QuoteFancy, https://quotefancy.com/quote/2435904/Earl-Nightingale-Successful-people-are-not-without-problems-They-re-simply-people-who-ve#:~:text=Earl%20Nightingale%20Quote%3A%20%E2%80%9CSuccessful%20people,learned%20to%20solve%20their%20problems.%E2%80%9D, accessed August 24, 2021.

11

Directional Influences—Part II

Helping Students Tackle Social Media and Their Inner Voice

Now, we move on to the last half of my directional influences list, starting with the parent/teacher dynamic. This section begins with a story that involves a teacher who slugs it out in the trenches each day. Let's call her Ms. Brave. As I typed this, a hailstorm was swirling around her. She teaches students with autism. There is rarely a day where she doesn't endure being kicked, bit, spat on, or getting a clump of her hair yanked out.

Despite the many challenges, she loves these kids…100%. In a minute, you will appreciate how deeply rooted that affection is. One swirling storm that especially tested her began when a student above her grade level got transferred into her classroom. Apparently, his other teacher could not handle his behavior issues. (If you are new to education, this type of thing happens quite frequently.) Just a few short days after entering her classroom, he went ballistic. I know that is not a technical term, but that is the way it sounded to me. He stood up, got in a fighting stance with Ms. Brave, and started wailing away.

She was left with no recourse but to follow standard, approved procedure, using a soft floor mat to corral him into one location so no other children got hurt by his outburst. This meant

DOI: 10.4324/9781003374497-11

Ms. Brave put herself in harm's way. Throughout this process, she was bitten and punched numerous times. He kept swinging and hitting the mat as well, which caused a bruise on his arm. Eventually after some additional support came, the student calmed down.

This was just a somewhat typical day for Ms. Brave, until ... the next day. The storm continued to worsen when the boy's mother arrived and accused Ms. Brave of bruising her son's wrist. This mother knew full well what her son was capable of, but she was looking for someone to blame. Did Ms. Brave show the mother all the bruises and bite marks that her son had inflicted? No. She listened to the mother and calmly explained what happened, all the while internalizing the negative attitude spewing from this woman.

Ms. Brave's frustration was overwhelming. Before she even realized it, she was defending her love and compassion for her students to the school's administration. Mind you, they were fully supportive of her and understood the situation. Some of them even helped to intervene, yet Ms. Brave felt like she had to defend herself verbally to those who would listen—not because she did anything wrong, but because this parent got under her skin.

This is just the bare bones of the story. When Ms. Brave shared it with me, I listened intently for as long as I could. When I couldn't listen to her self-mutilation any longer, I abruptly interrupted:

> I have to stop you right there. You can no longer give this woman this much control over you. You are a great teacher. Everyone knows that. But you are beating yourself up over some mother who has a lousy attitude and no clue what she's talking about. You are better than that. Do not give her that much control!

I stayed on my soap box for a bit longer. When I finally stopped, she calmly said, "Thank you." The good news is, I spoke to Ms. Brave the next day and she had slept well the night before for the first time since the episode. She approached me a few days later to say was going to be more forgiving to herself in other areas of her life. Now that's what I call an attitude change!

Choking on Words

Have you ever choked on your own words when someone feeds them right back to you? Three days after I shared my message with Ms. Brave, she did just that. At the time of writing this, I am not on any social media platforms... not one (for many reasons, but I won't bore you with the details). Keep that in mind as I describe this next event.

It took place on a Saturday night; I was working as a strolling magician at a local venue, walking table to table as I performed. A jovial venue with plenty of music, food, and drinks, it represented a breeding ground for great, up-close reactions to my magic act. Toward the end of the night, one of the employees shot a short video of me performing for two young kids and posted it on social media. The next day, I received a message from the person who had plugged me into working at the venue. Since I am not on social media, he shared a response to the video from some other magician. It read:

> That 'ahhhhaaha' and pointing at the end is really condescending ... kids or not ... just an observation.

"Immediately, I found myself frustrated. As the day went on, my frustration turned into irritation. None of it made sense to me. I didn't understand why that person would propagate such negativity. More importantly, I didn't understand why I let it bother me so much! Indeed, that bugged me the most. I began defending myself to anyone who would listen, including Ms. Brave. She patiently listened for a while, then she did the unthinkable: shoved my words back down my throat. She told me I could not beat myself up over it and to not give this guy so much control over me. She was 100% correct! I gained peace by thinking how sad it was that the commentator had nothing better to do than to demean another artist. Why add negativity to the world when we don't have to?

Without a doubt, this was not the first negative comment this individual has thrown into the vast world of social media. The unfortunate thing about this example is the poster of negative comments doesn't realize the long-term impact he is having on himself. Even if he was spot on about my performance, he only reinforced his own poor attitude. His habit of posting negative comments will snowball. By habitually focusing on and pointing out the negative, this habit will turn into a ritual, which will morph into his character. Once that happens, he will live his life in a dark rainstorm of negativity. He is programming his RAS to pinpoint and highlight the negative in life.

This is the world young learners are living in; people hiding behind small screens, casting judgment on everyone out there. They are bullying, judging, and hating in ways they would never dream of doing face-to-face. Our students face ridicule like no other generation before them—likes, dislikes, thumbs up, thumbs down, subscribe, unsubscribe—that is a lot to process on a daily basis. In one study I saw, 26% of respondents have let a negative comment ruin their day [1]. I would venture to guess it is actually way higher. Life is too short to allow people we do not even know, rob us of a day we could be using to achieve our goals. This is yet another reason to equip students with the knowledge of how to monitor and change their attitude.

Student/Social

> "Someone's opinion of you does not have to define your reality."
>
> —Les Brown [2]

This reality is a prime reason for this next Bowl Meeting question:

Bowl Meeting: How Do You Handle Negative Feedback on Social Media?

After the above-mentioned incident, this question burdened me the rest of the weekend. How do students cope in a constant cyberspace and social media barrage of negativity? I shared the previous story with them and told them I wanted to develop a procedure for students to follow when (not if) they encounter negative feedback via social media. Many of the students said, "I ignore them," or, "They are just people online."

One student opened up and gave us a glimpse of how she processes this, saying, "I am already hard on myself. Therefore, it really impacts me. It fuels me even more to be hard on myself." I asked what she does when that happens. She replied, "I just focus on the positivity around me and the people who I am closest to." What a great outlook!

Isn't it human nature to focus on the one negative while surrounded by a thousand positives? Interstate 4 is a notorious stretch of highway where I live. You pretty much have to follow it when you want to go anywhere in Orlando. On top of that, it seems like it is always under construction. It is funny to think that on a twenty-minute drive down I-4, you might encounter a thousand cars. Nine hundred ninety-nine are driving just fine, but just one cuts you off and it's: "Oh man! I hate I-4! These people don't know how to drive!" I have often reacted that way. But the reality is that only one of those thousand drivers demonstrated selfish driving habits. Those are not bad odds. It takes just a slight attitude adjustment, and we can see the 999 and ignore the one. Our RAS can help us do that.

Learning how to govern their response and attitude to negative comments on social media is important for our learners to grasp. (Clearly, I must learn it too.) Through my discussion with my students, we developed mindsets that we need to practice on a regular basis to maintain a thumbs-up attitude when living in a thumbs-down world.

1. If you know you are a sensitive person, then don't post anything, or at least turn off the replies.
2. Follow people you know. It is way more difficult to serve up that negativity to someone with whom you have a real, face-to-face relationship.
3. Before posting anything, anticipate negative comments and plan how you will process them.
4. Remember, the faceless people commenting online most likely have low self-esteem and think poorly about themselves.
5. Pity them. They are drowning in a world of negativity. Misery loves company. Don't swim with them—that's what they want.
6. (You gotta say this next one while pumping your fists and banging on your chest.) Don't give them power or permission to hurt you!

It's funny. When I shared the list of six steps for dealing with social media criticism with one of my classes, a student got heated about #4, saying, "That is just stupid. Just ignore them."

"How do you ignore them?" I replied politely.
After fumbling through a response, he said in frustration, "You just do."

He continued to rant about the stupidity and worthlessness of number four. Yet, he never articulated how to "just ignore them." You would never guess what happened. As he continued, no fewer than five students jumped to the defense of that step. While he never backed down, that reinforced its validity. Perhaps, that student does not need to use number four as a way to combat negative feedback. That is perfectly okay. You might have nineteen students in your class who can manage their attitudes despite negative comments, so this message might just be for the one who can't. However, that one is so important. Share all these tips with your class. They have the ability to revolutionize a student's outlook. Like so many aspects about attitude, these things must be practiced.

In a discussion with a friend of mine, Andy, we mulled over the role social media plays in a student's life. Andy brought up that learning to cope with the negativity in social media at an early age can help prepare students for their career. A graphic designer, he developed some of the graphics for this book. He described how so often he will submit a design for a job, but it gets shot down right away; his work is under a continual barrage of scrutiny. Therefore, Andy must handle the negativity at many stops along the journey of producing the final product.

This is a valuable career connection that this topic can have for our students. Coping with negativity from social media can translate into better coping with scrutiny in the workforce. As I watched countless airline passengers slugging flight attendants or each other in post-lockdown days, I couldn't help thinking a bunch of people need this kind of training.

We must recognize that we are going to bask in the sun some days, and be tossed against the waves in others. We must remember we have the ability to control those waves of emotions that destroy the foundation of our attitudes. Getting that control takes time, effort, patience, and endurance. Take my word for it: it is worth it in the end. Therefore, why not begin equipping our students with these skills earlier in life? Our role as educators is to equip our students to be problem-solvers so they can have more than a fighting chance at success. They will have a map to achieving it.

Student/Student

Up to this point I have looked at some of the connections between students, parents, teachers, and social influences, in relation to a student's attitude. What I haven't mentioned yet is how students influence their own attitude. While I mentioned self-talk earlier in the question about emotional success, I want to take a closer look at how their viewpoints regarding fear, failure, and the label "average" can severely impact their attitudes and success.

When analyzing the influences that impact our learners, it is imperative to acknowledge the number one poison of propagating progress: a person's inner voice. This point is a reminder that we are either our greatest champion or our greatest obstacle. It all depends on our inner voice. If we say, "I can't do 'this,'" or, "I can't accomplish 'that,'" then our inner conversation has just talked us out of any motivation we had and any chance we had of accomplishing our goal.

The key for our learners is to recognize that inner voice and either demolish it or develop it. They need to recognize whose "voice" is associated with the message they are so apt to follow. Is it their teacher who has championed them, or the voice of all those naysayers and negative commentators trying to bring them down? Often, it could be the voice of a parent or someone else close to them. No matter what the source, we have to have to change the message of our learners' inner voice. Read on to learn more about dealing with failure.

☑ Key Takeaways

1. As educators, we have to proactively regulate how much we allow a parent's attitude to influence us, especially when their attitude is negative.
2. Learning how to govern their response and attitude to negative comments on social media is important for our learners to grasp.
3. The key for our learners is to recognize their inner voice and either demolish it or develop it.

💭 Points to Ponder—Chapter 11

1. How much have you allowed a social media comment impact your day?
2. Quiz your students: Find out how long they spend on social media a day.

References

1. George McCarriston, "One-quarter of Americans Say a Negative Internet Comment Has Ruined Their Day," *YouGovAmerica*, September 7, 2017, https://today.yougov.com/topics/lifestyle/articles-reports/2017/09/07/26-americans-say-negative-internet-comment-has-rui

2. "Les Brown: Quotable Quote," *GoodReads*, https://www.goodreads.com/quotes/363985-someone-s-opinion-of-you-does-not-have-to-become-your, accessed August 17, 2021.

12

Overcoming Defeat

Teaching Your Students to Fail Their Way to Success

One of my favorite Bowl Meeting discussions revolves around the two-part question:

Bowl Meeting: How Have You Failed in the Last Week? The Last Month?

There is just no way to address attitude, success, and goal setting without discussing fear and failure. Our students need to be taught how to appropriately view "failure" so they can understand how "failure" can reshape their lives. How do you build a muscle? You must tear it down first, then rebuild it so it becomes stronger, bigger, and better.

Sometimes dreams, goals, and aspirations must be torn down so they can grow larger than we ever imagined. Formal education rarely teaches the necessity of failure. If a student fails on an assignment or a project, it gets logged into the gradebook and the lesson ceases. However, shouldn't that failure be used as a teaching moment? Far too often, formal education paints a linear picture of success. Starting in kindergarten, students begin

DOI: 10.4324/9781003374497-12

jumping through the hoops, all the way through to college, and then a great career is their reward. Essentially, a straight line with stops along the way, with ultimate victory awaiting at the end.

The challenge with such idealism is it is simply not realistic. It doesn't take into consideration all the other options, such as technical college, trade schools, and independent learning, an ever-increasing reality in an always-on, always-connected world. In addition, it does not include all the other facets of success I previously mentioned. The road to success has peaks, valleys, and movement that is linear, horizontal, backward, and at times stationary. That road looks more like the wave-like curving road example I mentioned previously.

If we develop in our students the ability to look at all the peaks, valleys, and small successes and failures as necessary moments in their journey toward success, they can more deeply appreciate this point and look at each moment of failure as a learning experience.

Fail your way to success.

Once, while waiting at the airport, I met a US Marine named Josh. I took this opportunity to ask him what he had learned from the military about failure. He said in basic training the drill sergeants ensure you repeatedly fail. He said no matter what you did, they made sure you failed. If you met the goal, then they just raised the bar. He described it as a way of building your tolerance of failure. Not to get comfortable with it, but rewiring your mind to get up and go again—no matter what. Essentially, failure is a mindset. It is only failure if you let it stop you.

I have experienced failure in my professional life, personal life, and financial life. I was almost fired from my job as a news reporter because of my attitude toward my boss. I am divorced. I bought a condo in 2005 and sold it in 2018 for ten thousand dollars less than I paid for it. The list could go on and on. For years, I thought I was the sum of my failures. It wasn't until my attitude changed that I can now see those things made me stronger, bigger, and better. I viewed my failures as a 50-foot uns-calable barrier, instead of as a trampoline to the next level of life. Students need to hear this discussion. They are constantly rated with a pass/fail standard. We must teach them how to view fail-ures in life as a trampoline to greater success!

Failing Forward

In listening to a podcast about success, I discovered a gem of an interview. Sara Blakely is the founder of a billion-dollar business called SPANX, which is a women's apparel line. Her extreme animation and vivacity are evident throughout the interview. In discussing her childhood, she shares how her father would frequently ask her, "What have you failed at this week?" She describes that he would almost be disappointed if she hadn't failed at anything. His lesson to her was how to find value from failure and how to learn something new each time she failed [1]. Given the right approach; this is a great question you can peri-odically ask your classes. It could even be a Bowl Meeting dis-cussion question.

My school is a visual and performing arts magnet, which affords me the ability to teach a magic class. It is the best speech class students will ever take. They learn how to perform the mechanics of tricks, but those lessons are sandwiched around much more valuable lessons, such as how to approach strangers and how to be more engaging when speaking publicly.

One of the greatest fears when performing magic is messing up a trick. It is not a matter of *if* you will mess up a trick, but *when*. To this day I still mess them up. However, I have taught myself and my students to celebrate those failures because they teach something valuable. I have taught them that when they do mess up, just think to yourself, "Yes! I just learned something!" By rewiring their brains and viewpoint, they can view mistakes and failures as catalysts of learning. This is a technique I have adopted in my personal life, although it takes loads and loads of practice.

In the summer of 2018, I was invited to the world-famous Magic Castle in Los Angeles. Located in Hollywood, it is a clubhouse for magicians that only admits members and their guests. In the just-ended school year, I had taught a student with a famous magician father named Michael Ammar. He was performing at the Magic Castle and invited me to come get a glimpse into that exclusive world. Once I did, I was hooked. I had to perform at the Magic Castle. Immediately, I jumped into action and established a goal to perform there within eighteen months. This meant I had to develop a 22-minute show, record a video of it, and submit it to the Castle's decision-makers.

This proved to be a much more arduous task than it may sound. This marked the first time I had ever recorded a video of a magic performance. While not a complete disaster, it was a learning experience—particularly of my constant motion. I had to learn to center myself and not move so much. The next time I recorded a show, I performed for a group of teachers after school, first asking the receptionist to not make any announcements over the intercom. I am sure you can guess what happened. Halfway through the show, fuzzy sounds crackled from the speaker followed by: "Would Mister So-and-So please come to the front office?"

It's the story of my existence. Time and time again (ten by my count), when I recorded a performance, something went wrong. It was always something beyond my control. Seriously, I am running out of places to try. Yet, each time, I have taken something away from the "failure" and improved my show. I almost welcome the mess-ups! At the time I write these words, I have missed my deadline, but I am not giving up.

Here is yet another example related to this goal that caused a setback. When I was finally able to record a halfway decent production, Michael took my video out to the Magic Castle to personally hand it over to the powers-that-be. The only problem was, the moment his plane landed in Los Angeles, the whole state of California went into lockdown because of the coronavirus pandemic. Once things eventually calm down and normalcy is restored, I will storm forward with my goal. My students know this story. In fact, I have even performed the show for them. I must lead by example and fail my way to success.

Reframing Thinking

There are so many circumstances in life that require reframing our thinking about failure, besides just the goals we have set. Have you ever met a cancer survivor? Isn't it astounding the battle they have gone through? More often than not, they come out of this with a different view of life. They didn't let the failure of their cells define their lives. Please understand I am not being flippant with the challenges faced by cancer sufferers. My grandfather lost his battle with cancer, but my mother was a two-time cancer survivor.

In addition, since 2004 I have gone to an Orlando kids' hospital called Arnold Palmer Hospital for Children. I perform magic once a week for pediatric patients, some of whom are battling cancer. It is the most rewarding thing I do; what I learn from the patients is so mind bogglingly (is that a word?) amazing. It is so astonishing how a child who is bald from chemotherapy, or who has burn marks on her skin from radiation, can laugh at my magic. Now, that is an astounding attitude. They could drown themselves in the failure of their body, but they choose to find a way to laugh.

Likewise, whether we want them to or not, failures and challenges will come our students' way. What are you doing to prepare learners for them when they arrive? By challenging them with the question "How have you failed in the last week (or month)?", you can help them continue their reflective journey. The important thing is to follow up that question with: "What did you learn from your failure?" Sometimes the lesson does not reveal itself immediately. However, this line of questioning primes our learners to always be on the lookout for what they can learn from failure.

This reality is behind another Bowl Meeting prompt I like to pose:

Bowl Meeting: Tell Us about a Time When You Were Really Embarrassed

To return to the Sara Blakely interview I mentioned earlier, she does a tremendous job of tying the concept of fear and failure together, boiling it down to the fact that the fear of failure is actually the fear of embarrassment; the fear of what people might think about you. As I meditated about helping students overcome such fears, I got the idea for the Wall of Enhancing Embarrassments.

After another Bowl Meeting where the students describe their embarrassing moment, I extend a challenge. If they submit a video or get up in front of the class and do something embarrassing—within reason and school regulations—they will get their name added to the Wall. The "wall" is really just a small strip of bulletin board paper with a small sign that states Wall of Enhancing Embarrassments. Students jump at the chance to get their name up there. When they add their name to the wall it is one small step closer for these students in overcoming their fear of failures and embarrassments.

I launch this challenge by doing something embarrassing. For example, I may share with the students how when I cook, I sing stupid songs about the food I am cooking. The songs are always unique to what I am making. For example, when I make guacamole, I sing a song that goes like this: "Guac, guac, guac, guacamooooleee. Guac, guac, guac, guacamooooleee." While I realize the song will not transfer well into print, trust me—it sounds pretty awful.

Accompanied by the dance moves that I do, this leads to quite an embarrassing moment. I share this with my students in an effort to get them to realize that being embarrassed in front of your peers (and more importantly, failing in front of your peers) is not the end of the world. Plus, embarrassing moments make for a great story! After breaking the ice with my foolishness, I challenge them to do the same in the next thirty days. Among the things they have done is videoing themselves walking around with toilet paper attached to the seat of their shorts, or dressing up to perform their version of a Carmen Miranda! (That is the dancer with fruit on her head more often called the Chiquita banana lady.)

This activity makes for exciting and amusing moments while empowering students to break out of the bondage of fear and insecurity. It is imperative that students give themselves permission to be laughed at and even to fail. By redefining a learner's perspective of failing, they have a greater chance of obtaining their ultimate success down the road. Failures help them learn the things not to do so, when the time is right, they can succeed at what their heart desires. The appropriate viewpoint of failures also can help them conquer our next topic of discussion.

Formidable Fears

Another Bowl Meeting question that usually stirs considerable discussion is:

Bowl Meeting: What Fears Do You Have That Would Stop You from Achieving Your Definition of Success?

Now, if you have never watched a little kid ski, it is a sight to behold. I'm not talking about the ones on the bunny slope. I mean the ones who grew up skiing, who will whip around you on the slope, and do teddy bears off every bump down the run. Those kids. The fearless ones. Why are they so fearless? Because they learned to ski at an early age, they have already faced pain. They tear down that mountain because they have no fear. They are familiar with the maneuvers needed to navigate the terrain. They know how to get up, dust off the snow, and continue down the mountain.

One of the biggest extinguishers of a person's burning passion is fear: fear of ridicule, fear of rejection, fear of failure. Teaching someone the right questions and having the right attitude is no different than a child learning how to ski. If we begin early on in a person's journey to teach these ideas, they will know the maneuvers needed to successfully navigate life's terrain. However, if we neglect teaching these things, when it is time for someone to set out on their trek to success, fear will overpower them, stifle them, and eventually crush them. This is why we need to equip our learners with these skills.

To really get to the heart of the matter and peel back the layers of fear requires a person to take an inventory of how fear has played a part in their lives, even as a young child. In the previous example of the fearless child snow skiing, I alluded to how we can do fearless things as a child since we were never "taught" to fear them. What happens, though, when we adopt a fear as a child, when many fears gain a foothold? We can carry into adulthood a perceived fear and yet not recognize how it continues to impact us.

A great example of how fears can start in childhood popped up when I asked someone close to me named Chelsea about one of her earliest memories of fear. Her response captures the point I am making. She described how, at the age of eight or nine, she was crawling through some bushes because, she said, "I liked digging through the dirt and looking for bugs." As she slowly continued her journey, she found something she hadn't bargained for—a wolf spider's nest. If you are unfamiliar with what a wolf spider looks like, think of Aragog from *Harry Potter* (just not that big). And, of course, think of all of Aragog's children falling and crawling all over her. As panic and fear shot through her body, thorns from the rose bush delayed her mad dash out of there. Once free of the plant's snare, bloody and covered in spiders, she darted back to her house. That built the foundation of her fear of spiders, which she carries with her to this day.

Innate or Identity

Fear of spiders is one of two types of fears I would like to dissect: (1) innate fears; and (2) identity fears.

An innate fear is like the one I just described about spiders. An innate fear involves perceived physical pain or harm, whether that involves something like heights, snakes, or darkness. Identity fears morph into various forms as we age. They revolve around your identity and are connected to fears of being judged.

This connects to Sara Blakely's comment that the fear of failure is the fear of embarrassment, which, at its root, is fear of what people will think about you. Fear of public speaking is a great example. The fear of being rejected or being wrong both come from the same place. Fear of embarrassment and humiliation from your peers stems from human beings having a desire to be part of a tribe and a sense of belonging. I would like to progress what Blakely said just a step or two further. I propose the following:

> fear of failure → fear of embarrassment → fear of what people think → fear of not being accepted → fear of being alone

In this flow chart, the fear of not being accepted and the fear of being alone play a greater role in people's lives than most will admit. Looking back at these two responses given by learners when asked what they worry about the most, the correlation is quite apparent.

1. Losing all my friends and not being able to make new ones.
2. Losing my family because of something I have done.

Students gave these kinds of responses more than once. They surface regularly in discussions with learners. Apparently, my students are not alone. In one article I read, nearly one in three adults admitted they feared being alone [2]. It is not a stretch to see how the fear of being alone festers into a fear of failure. By leading the learner to the root of their fears, they can begin to face them more rationally. Once they do that, they can begin to conquer them. This is a prime reason for challenging your learners to participate in the Wall of Enhancing Embarrassments. It will help them build confidence that if they do something silly or outside their comfort zone, they will not lose their friends.

> *Fear is the fertilizer of excuses. Time to pull up the weeds.*

As you can imagine, while writing this book, I grappled with such fears as: What if they think my writing style is too casual and discount my credibility? What if it doesn't have the impact on educators and students that I hope it will? My passion and belief in the messages contained in this book wouldn't let me stop. I refused to allow my fears to overpower my passion. I firmly believe this message can impact millions of students. Throughout the writing of this book, rarely did I encounter a person with whom I did not share what I am learning and writing. That is how passionate I am about this project. Through these conversations, it came to my attention how many adults do not understand the importance of these lessons. They are letting fear stand in the way of their success and they don't even realize it. The fear propagates excuses.

To open the discussion with learners about the difference between innate and identity fears, you can always pose the question mentioned before about one of their earliest memories of fear. This will allow them to share their innate fears. Plus, you will get a laugh or two from their stories. The important thing is to use that as a teaching moment and describe how their examples are innate fears. Then, use that to transition to the identity fears and a full Bowl Meeting around the question: What fears do you have that would stop you from achieving your success? Read on to learn more about the enemy of success: settling for "average."

✅ Key Takeaways

1. How a student processes failure can determine their successes in life. Reframe failure.
2. Fear of embarrassment can cause a crippling fear in students. Reframe embarrassment.
3. Fail your way to success.

💭 Points to Ponder—Chapter 12

1. Is there a fear you have that has put up a roadblock to your success?

2. Historically, what fears have you encountered your students possess?

References

1. "SPANX Founder Sara Blakely on Overcoming Fear of Failure in Business," *YouTube*, June 23, 2020, https://www.youtube.com/watch?v=9JrAojUqMvQ
2. Taryn Hillin, "1 in 3 U.S. Adults Admit They Fear Being Alone, Survey Finds," *HuffPost*, February 24, 2014, updated December 6, 2017, https://www.huffpost.com/entry/relationship-fears-_n_4826875

13

"Average" Is a Curse Word

Pushing Students to Purge This Toxic Mindset

Regulating fear and recognizing the benefits of failure fall within the student/student attitude influence, meaning both fear and failure can be regulated within the student mindset. There is one other condemning mindset that plagues our students—the mindset of "average." To me, average is 100% a curse word. The attitude of average is a toxic state of mind that must be modified. Who wants to be average? Look average? Feel average? Live average?

Now, I am not talking about an arbitrary grade tacked on to a class assignment, nor am I downplaying a person's abilities. Students must conduct a self-evaluation of their own performance to determine if they gave an average effort. Did they truly give it their all? Did they "leave it all on the field?" Did they sincerely give their utmost focus and attention? If they did, then they are above average and will receive above-average results. Did they cut corners? Lose focus? Play around instead of working? Then they will wallow in the muck and mud of an average life—indefinitely.

My high school chemistry class was the hardest class I have ever taken. My teacher flat out told us she was getting us ready for college. She wasn't lying. We would spend about thirteen

DOI: 10.4324/9781003374497-13

hours a week outside of class, doing homework and typing up lab reports, and then be lucky to get a "C" on them. No one could let her small stature and endearing face fool them. Let me assure you, she beat the mess out of us (figuratively speaking). And I loved her for it. I finished that year with a "C" in her class. Was that average in my mind? No way. I gave more than an "average" effort and was proud of the results.

It is time to kill the average attitude in our students. Would you believe, when discussing this topic in class, one student said, "I don't try hard because it's just seventh grade. It doesn't matter." I had to check my attitude rather quickly before I responded. Despite attempting multiple angles to persuade him otherwise, he stuck to his guns.

Unless that attitude changes, he will not be pleased with the long-term results. He is establishing habits that will turn into rituals. Those rituals will become a lifestyle. When things get tough, he will fall back on those dismissive, poor attitudes because that is the foundation he poured. We play how we practice, and we practice how we play. This will be a hard lesson for him to learn down the road. I am not giving up on him, but he has to establish better work habits of his own accord if he hopes to ever shed that attitude. I can only present options to him; he must be his own catalyst of change.

> *Success is so difficult because the reason NOT to do something is so easy. I hate being average.*

Average is a forsaken word that we need to strike from our vocabulary. The "average attitude mindset" is a disease that spreads quicker and easier than a common cold. A cold can take 24- to 72 hours for its incubation period, while symptoms of an average attitude can surface within seconds. If you don't believe me, walk into work on a Monday and ask someone about their weekend. A far-too-common answer: "It was too short." Bam! You just got infected. Before you know it, you have joined in that conversation. That is an average attitude. An average attitude within a group of friends can strangle the life out of the party.

An average attitude will always have a reason to NOT do something while it ignores 20 reasons for doing it.

Thank God It's Monday

One day in class, I heard a student say (as so many have said in countless workplaces), "Thank God it's Friday." This phrase got me to thinking. I don't want to live a life that I wish away until the next weekend or the next vacation. Nor do I want my learners to live like that. This student's statement prompted me to get on my soapbox and have a short discussion with the rest of my classes that day. What an awful way to live life wanting nothing more than to get away from your job or obligations.

I am sure you have come across someone who has said on a Tuesday or Wednesday that they can't wait until Friday. Why not have the attitude that is grateful for it being Tuesday because you can work on something that day that will get you closer to obtaining your goals? Even start saying, "Thank God it's Monday!" Then charge into the week eager to take on the world. Don't get me wrong, there is nothing wrong with being excited about an event in your life, but life is too short to wish it away. The TGIF mentality is a symptom of a toxic, average attitude.

Let's purge the attitude of "average" from our students' minds and vocabulary. Once we do that, they will start to receive higher gains in all endeavors in life. My students always ask, "Okay, Mr. Yuhasz, we are done with the project; what do we do now?" I simply respond, "Make it better." I put it back in their hands to determine if they have given their best effort. They do not like it, but they can take ownership when they take stock of their efforts. I try to raise the bar of their expectations and work ethic. Let's chop down the attitude that enables them to be architects of average and morph them into architects of amazing!

Before someone accuses me of climbing too high on my soapbox, I must confess that teachers are just as guilty of harboring an "average" attitude. Have you ever called yourself "just" a teacher? Or maybe you have heard another teacher say that. This is a symptom of an average attitude. For some reason in their

> *From the points where you give me hundreds to the place where you say "you are not done so make it better" these things make me try harder in life and in school. Because you make me try harder and you teach us amazing things*

FIGURE 13.1 A student's great response to being pushed to raise the level of work.

minds, some educators think they rank below other career fields. This is simply not true. Teachers are highly educated managers. How many business managers out there have direct influence over as many people as a teacher does?

In an average year I have 150 students. As I write this, I have 175 students on my roster. That is a small business I am managing—right out of my classroom! This means I am the CEO, CFO, and COO of room 240 at my school. Even if you are teaching elementary school with 18 to 25 students, you possess amazing managerial skills. Please stop yourself or any other teacher from using the term "just" a teacher. It is a toxic mindset. If you do not believe in the value of what you do, how will the students?

At a training seminar not too long ago, I overheard two teachers talking (I didn't know either one of them). When one teacher asked the other what she was getting her master's degree in, her response was, "Just education." I literally interrupted them to say, "It is not 'just' education. That is a great degree!" While she quickly backpedaled and apologized, I didn't want an apology. I wanted her to realize the tremendous value she is adding to our world, but it was like she was almost embarrassed about it. If we wish to make the changes in education that are needed, we need to not say, "I am *just* a teacher," but to proclaim, "I am a teacher. Hear me roar!" We have to kill the average mindset in ourselves and our students.

Purging a Mindset

There is such a tremendous value in students learning at a young age that they should purge the "average" mindset, along with my previous points about learning that they can turn failure into victories and overcome their fears. All three of these categories can have a damaging effect on a person's attitude; they are also lessons most of us have had to learn more than once. I certainly have. It is important to remember we can't control the wind or the waves, but we can find a way to make the best of them.

> When everything seems to be going against you, remember that the airplane takes off against the wind, not with it.
> —Henry Ford [1]

Speaking of flying, the first thing a pilot checks before even planning a flight is the weather conditions. Often, they will look at them days in advance. The type of certification the pilot has will determine their ability to fly. Visibility must be a certain amount, along with the height of the cloud cover, before taking off. This can determine their cruising altitude.

Just as it is important for pilots to check the altitude of the clouds before rolling down the runway, so a person should check their emotional altitude before rolling out of bed each day. It can take just moments to reflect on how they are starting their day. When a person identifies negative attitudes at the onset of their day, they have a better chance of altering those attitudes by taking a short emotional assessment. Then throughout the day, by conducting periodic emotional altitude checks, they are more likely to take corrective measures to maintain an emotionally high altitude. Students can learn how to conduct a "pre-flight" checklist each day.

I find it immensely beneficial when I recognize my emotions—especially my attitude—are turning sour to pause and visualize almost floating above myself. Then, I "look" down and start evaluating why I am having such an emotional response to the circumstance. I quickly evaluate what I can control about the situation and what I cannot. Ninety-nine percent of the time, all I can control is my response. After identifying the catalysts for the bad attitude and recognizing I can't control the circumstances, I am left with one route to take: change my attitude. The beauty of this practice is once I take that "aerial" view of the circumstance and identify triggers for my attitude, more often than not my attitude begins to change for the better.

Thus, another of my Bowl Meeting discussions:

Bowl Meeting: Describe a Time in Your Life You Had a Bad Attitude About Doing Something, But After All Was Said and Done, It Turned Out Okay

As you can imagine, I get all kinds of responses. Figure 13.2 shows just a couple examples:

> One of my new really good friends I was told had issues and problems with someone i'm very close with and I hated them until we talked and she turned out to be truly amazing!

> I didn't really think greatly of my dad's girlfriend but she is actually a good person

FIGURE 13.2 These students learned how to change their attitudes.

Hopefully, you can see how this prompt can lead to tremendous class discussions and give you a better glimpse into the challenges your students face. Living in central Florida, a lot of responses have to do with the first time they rode a roller coaster. Fear of something can always impact a person's attitude, but I try to get the student to really reflect on WHY they had a bad attitude in the first place. I want them to identify their emotional anchor.

Following the Evidence

It is important for students to think about the way they think and dissect whether there was/is an underlying issue they have anchored to, leading to their negative attitude. One example comes to mind when a girl shared that she didn't like going to the beach because the first time she went she stepped on a shark. She wasn't hurt, just badly rattled. I used that opportunity to discuss how attitudes can be anchored by emotions or evidence. In this circumstance, she had a small piece of data and anchored a large emotion to it. I was proud she overcame that attitude and has since gone and enjoyed the beach! (And no, people who live in Florida are not always attacked by sharks and alligators.)

Sometimes, however, the evidence can lead to strong emotions. Another student said he had a bad attitude about going out on a boat with his family. When he tried it a second time, though, he had fun. When I asked him why he had a bad attitude about it, he told me the first time he got sick. Naturally, I asked, "Did you get sick the second time?" Sure enough, he did. No wonder he had a bad attitude. Who could blame him?

These are just "light" examples of how a student's attitude can be anchored to something with or without supporting evidence. If students can learn with smaller examples how to look for evidence that constructs their attitude, then they can do it when it comes to more significant areas in their lives. Learning how to reconstruct their attitude can be a game-changer.

The topic opens the floodgates for me to discuss education. Not sure about you, but not all my students love coming to school every day. (Of course, they love your class. It is the other classes that are the problem.) I want them to understand how their attitude and their approach to education can determine how successful they are.

Students need to hear this: We can't control our family, friends, neighbors, spouses, or teachers, but we can control our attitude and reaction to them. This includes students' attitudes towards education. Do they dislike math because of a subpar teacher? Maybe one who told them they would never use this information? Is history challenging because they never understood its value? Does "education" as a whole lack value in their home? Is it worth taking the time to uncover your students' hidden attitudes toward education? That can lead you to understand their motivation or lack thereof. Unburying their anchors can also help reprogram their RAS.

> Life is 10 percent what happens to me and 90 percent how I react to it.
>
> —Chuck Swindoll [2]

Throughout this discussion, I encourage my students to try and anchor their attitudes to a positive time and not just negative experiences. This way, the next time something comes their way they have a sour attitude about, they can reflect on the past and recognize things can turn out well in the end. I also emphasize that having a negative attitude well supported with evidence is really okay, since this can lead to positive life changes. A negative attitude toward a person who repeatedly wronged you can lead you to disassociating from that person.

After sharing this idea with my students, the next day a coworker greeted me warmly as she grinned from ear to ear. Her son, Isaac, was in my class. She told me despite her nagging him to ditch this negative friend he had in his life; he would not do it. She said whatever I talked about in class had him coming home and saying, "Mom, I don't think I am going to be friends with so-and-so." Now that is a victory! It really must take a village to raise a child.

Forming Perceptions

In navigating this discussion with my students, I describe to them how—at an early age—we begin to form perceptions of the world. Often, those perceptions wind up being walls we build around us. Then, by the time we are adults we have a boxed-in perception of the world. This enclosed view can limit us from experiencing life. Take, for example, this student's response in Figure 13.3.

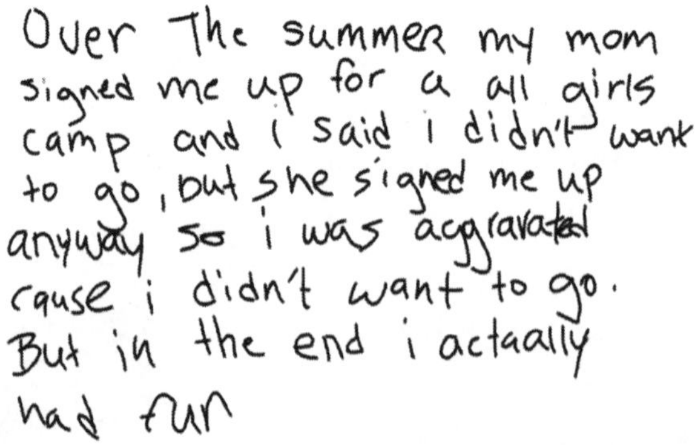

Over The summer my mom signed me up for a all girls camp and I said i didn't want to go, but she signed me up anyway so i was acgravated cause i didn't want to go. But in the end i actaally had fun

FIGURE 13.3 Student reflection on how they changed their perception of new experiences.

When I asked her the reason she didn't want to go, she responded, "I wanted to spend time with my friends." That seemed like a legitimate reason not to go, but I took the time to get her to recognize how trying new things can enhance her life. She just had to be willing to let go of some of her perceptions and negative anchors against doing something and be open-minded to new experiences in life. Essentially, I encourage her and all my students to be lifelong learners.

> Don't tie yourself to your history, tie yourself to your potential.
> —Stephen Covey [3]

What I enjoy about this topic of discussion with my students is when they begin to understand why "emotional health" needs to be part of their facets of success. I use this as a moment to refer back to the road map of success, which I discussed earlier. I strongly emphasize if they can learn to "un-anchor" negative attitudes early in life, they have a much greater chance of being emotionally successful as they get older.

Please understand, I am not being cavalier about how "easy" it is to "un-anchor" an attitude. It took me decades to shift mine, but it gives me the assurance that it can be done. Attitude can be trained, but it takes a purposeful effort to institute that change. How deeply anchored those emotions are tied to that negative attitude will determine how much effort has to be applied.

Sandwich of Gratitude

I use two more prompts with students to round out the topic of attitude. The first is:

Bowl Meeting: List Three Things You Are Grateful For

This sounds like a typical Thanksgiving Day discussion, but it needs to go deeper. The students need to be able to see how many wonderful things they have in their lives. As we discuss this prompt, I encourage my students to write down any others that pop into their minds. They can be small or large. I always give the example that I am super grateful I still have my hair. I know this is silly but growing up with a father who had a horseshoe head of hair, I was terrified of losing mine. The more the things along "silly" lines the students can recognize, the greater the pool they must pull from when times get tough. I just have my students fill in a chart that looks like a hamburger and create a sandwich of gratitude.

When teaching this prompt, students tend to list these top three items: friends, family, and pets. This is when I take the time to encourage them to tell their family and friends how much they appreciate them. This in turn can cause their loved ones to embrace gratitude, creating a big snowball. Students stacking their gratitude can keep things in perspective once trials come their way. After all, you can't have the right attitude unless you have plenty of gratitude.

The second, related prompt I often use is:

Bowl Meeting: Name Two Things You Are Successful at Right Now

This is such an important reflective question because it allows students to appreciate what they have already accomplished. Thus, it ties in perfectly to the sandwich of gratitude. For much of my life, I did not allow myself to appreciate the successes I had achieved. I had such a high standard set for myself of becoming an astronaut that nothing else along the journey seemed to matter. Naturally, this became a dismal time of my life. One day while talking with a friend named Meraux, he put it plainly: "You have to GIVE yourself your successes."

What a beautiful statement! I had to allow myself to embrace my accomplishments and celebrate my successes, no matter how small or big. This relates to the concept I reviewed earlier, about giving yourself permission to be laughed at and fail. Students must give themselves permission to celebrate their successes. This might seem like common sense, but as I like to say, "Common sense is not that common." If you have students who are wired like me—with lofty goals and very hard on themselves—then Meraux's statement will resonate with them; if they are ready to receive it. This prompt is a great way to teach students at an early age that it is good to celebrate their success and to "give themselves their successes."

✓ Key Takeaways

1. The "average attitude mindset" is a disease that spreads quicker and easier than a common cold.
2. We can't control our family, friends, neighbors, spouses, or teachers, but we can control our attitude and reaction to them.
3. Students can learn to anchor their attitudes to a positive time and not just negative experiences.
4. We all need to "give" ourselves our successes.

💭 Points to Ponder—Chapter 13

1. In what areas of your life do you have an "average mindset"?
2. How can you help your students better celebrate their successes?

References

1. "Henry Ford Quotes," *BrainyQuote*®, https://www.brainyquote.com/quotes/henry_ford_132651, accessed August 19, 2021.
2. "Charles R. Swindoll Quotes," *GoodReads*, https://www.goodreads.com/author/quotes/5139.Charles_R_Swindoll, accessed August 27, 2021.
3. "Stephen Covey Quotes," Quoteswise.com, http://www.quoteswise.com/stephen-covey-quotes-3.html, accessed August 27, 2021.

14

Lasting Attitude

Addressing a Pesky Negative Mindset with Your Students

Condensing all these ideas into a relatively modest space, it may seem like my class is just one big therapy session. In fact, I often get asked if that's what it's like. The answer is: no. I still teach plenty of content. Remember, 100% of my class passed their industry certification exam; all of them! By no means am I suggesting you turn your classroom into a psychologist's office. However, if we can instill in our students the meaningful concepts I explore here, we can be one step closer to helping them live richer, fuller lives.

When facilitating a discussion on "attitude" with your students, you most likely will face the question, "What do we do if we have a lasting bad attitude?"

Now, there aren't any magic pills one can take to change a negative attitude, but it starts with what we are putting into our brain and what we focus on. The brain is such an amazing machine, yet many people barely recognize its capabilities. Essentially, everything we feel is because our brain has released some chemical or neurotransmitter. (By the way, that is a bad line to mention on a first date. Just sayin'.) If our RAS is focused on the positive, then the brain releases mood-boosting endorphins

DOI: 10.4324/9781003374497-14

and serotonin more frequently. If our RAS focuses on the negative, then the brain produces far fewer of the previously mentioned "happy hormones." That said, our attitude is a reflection of the chemicals released, so doesn't it make sense to naturally alter them?

The mind is tremendously powerful. It can create thoughts and feelings about a person or situation that are completely untrue. Have you ever merely had a confrontation in your mind with someone and you physically got angry just by dwelling on it? I am the master of this! Recently, when I bought a new/used car, the dealer said they only had one key fob and they didn't have the ability to make another one. I stood my ground, but eventually I signed the papers.

Before I got home, in my head I was already accusing the salesperson of lying to me about the key. I went so far as to mentally compose a scathing email to them. Finally, I decided to just call the dealership to ask if they make replacement keys. I was determined to catch this sales guy in a lie. Sure enough, since I bought a Jeep from a Toyota dealership, they indeed did not have the ability to make the key fob I needed. (At this point, color me embarrassed—a deep shade of red, chagrin running down my cheeks, and feelings of foolishness coursing through my body.) I had allowed my emotions to run rampant and adversely affect me.

However, just because it was a figment of my imagination does not mean my body behaved like it was false. When I was younger, I created countless made-up arguments in my head, primarily directed at one antagonist. Time and time again, I would make myself physically angry just thinking about an altercation that never occurred. My mind interpreted these "synthetic experiences" as being real. This was not a pleasant time period in my life, since I allowed imaginary experiences to rob me of my joy.

Positive Impact

No doubt you and your students have endured such experiences. While the examples I gave are negative, synthetic experiences can also have a positive impact on your students' demeanors and attitudes. The brain releases chemicals—positive or negative—in accordance with those experiences. Fear leading up to an event can be a synthetic experience. Worry is a negative synthetic experience. Have your students experienced fear or worry prior to a test? The test hasn't even begun, and they are already suffering. Well, they can harness and channel these negative thoughts in a more positive way.

One thing you can have your students do to naturally alter those negative chemicals associated with real or fictitious experiences is have them move like they have confidence (remember when I mentioned how your physical state can impact your emotional state?). One year I had to facilitate my students taking an end-of-course algebra exam. Before starting, I had them raise their hands if they were nervous; a chorus of students quickly sounded: "I'm gonna fail." So, I told them to get up and stand like they were nervous about this test. Naturally, they stood there with heads down and shoulders slumped. Next, I told them to stand up like they were going to murder this test, advising: "Fake it if you have to. Then picture grabbing the test by its throat and ripping out its trachea."

A caution here: I am not promoting violence nor am I a violent person, but I wanted them to shake off those thoughts of negativity and replace them with a laugh in order to silence those negative thoughts. (And maybe replaced them with nightmares, but that is their parents' problem, right?) I remember the time I heard Magic Johnson discuss losing the NBA championship to the Bulls. Magic talked about how he knew when Michael Jordan walked in, this was a different player than he had faced in the past, all because of the way Jordan moved—with confidence. And your students can move with such confidence, too. This can alter your students' biochemistry and have an enormous, positive impact on their psyche.

Now, changing how they move is a short-term fix. As far as a longer-term fix, it comes down to what the brain has been disciplined to digest. Most of us are aware that if we consume the wrong foods, our body will not perform like it is capable of performing. Our brain is no different. If we are slamming in negativity, that's what will come out of it. When we focus on the negative, our RAS will identify more signs of negativity and feed them back to us.

Congested Road

If students continually surround themselves with people who are not uplifting and are terminally negative, they are congesting their road to success. Pessimism is as corrosive as stomach acid—and just as painful. Challenge students to surround themselves with people who will help them achieve their goals and maintain a positive attitude, since that can decongest that road. In many circumstances, the most toxic people might be members of their own family.

Therefore, introduce the option of listening to motivational podcasts or YouTube videos. They are free and in abundant supply. Students need a daily recharging of their attitude. They can listen to positive things while getting ready in the morning, eating breakfast, on the way to school, or during your class (well, maybe that last one could be a bit distracting). Anytime they can. This way, even if for just ten minutes a day, they can get a dose of positivity.

Every morning before I check emails or anything else, I listen to different uplifting speakers to ensure my attitude starts the day off on a high note. By feeding the brain positivity, it changes the Reticular Activating System to recognize positive things along their journey through life. Hence, a change in attitude follows, along with the release of those "positive feeling" chemicals called endorphins.

> *Devoting your mind to changing your attitude can redirect your life. It took me a lot of years to learn this one.*

One time a student approached me after class with a downtrodden stance; she looked as if she had lost a near and dear family member. Her head and shoulders hung as if they were weighed down by a sack of potatoes. Once she started talking, I learned she was upset about her grade in a language arts class. After listening to her repeatedly say, "I feel," or "I know," it dawned on me she had adopted a cellar-dwelling viewpoint on life. To help address her concerns, I laid out a plan of attack for her to bring up her grade.

This girl's problem centered on her inability to see past the current moment, let alone see far enough ahead to plan a solution to her problem. This reminded me how vital it is to teach learners to achieve a more aerial view of life. At the middle and high school level, students tend to have a short-term, narrow-minded focus. Today is a foreboding obstacle and tomorrow looks as far away as next year. Because of their "low" view of reality, small issues can escalate and exponentially compound into gigantic, life-altering events. They must view looming issues from a much higher perspective to avoid blowing them out of proportion.

As students grow and solve problems amid life's challenges, they will gain altitude in their viewpoint. However, you can help them achieve an elevated perspective more quickly by enlisting students in some form of community outreach. I know from personal experience that when my attitude (along with my perspective) begins to fly a bit too low, extending a hand to help others helps me to eliminate the "i" in attitude and broadens my perspective. The problems that seem so daunting to me may pale by comparison with those of someone struggling with serious health issues, or who fights to put food on the table, or who cares for a disabled child. We should encourage students to be part of some kind of community outreach. Their participation in such events can be life altering and, once again, release those aforementioned endorphins.

By understanding just some of the many influences that impact a student's attitude, we can begin to see the layers that make up a student's attitude. Then using the suggestions previously listed in this book and summarized in these next five steps, students can make tremendous strides in revamping their attitudes.

1. They must be fully committed to change.
2. Check their anchors. Identify the emotion or evidence to which their attitude is anchored. Weigh out the pros and cons of the opportunity and find a new place to anchor. (Essentially, reprogram their RAS to see the positive.)
3. In the short-term, fake an attitude change by changing how they move.
4. Be proactive. Prepare them for those events that can trigger a bad attitude by anticipating them. Then, map out how they can handle them.
5. For the long-term, they must alter what they are feeding their brains. Bad attitudes are toxic. Feed the mind good, positive food (goodbye Eeyore, hello Tigger).

By no means am I trying to trivialize the challenge of revamping someone's attitude. Nor am I saying simplistically: "Think positive, buddy!" It is way more than that. It took me decades to realize how to modify my own attitude. This is why I can share these things with my students. A healthy attitude toward life can allow a student to achieve more in the future than they can even fathom today. Combine the right attitude with the ability to make and achieve appropriate goals and a student will find many boundaries around them collapse as the opportunities abound.

As mentioned previously, during the process of writing this book, I underwent many challenges that could have negatively impacted my attitude, such as bulging and herniated discs in my neck and the sudden death of my mother. I was able to face such adversity because I put into practice the lessons I outline in this book. Daily, I am feasting and filling my brain with the words of positive speakers and other uplifting material. This way, when the famines of life occur, I will be ready. We shape our lives with our attitudes. That is exciting news because we actually have control of our attitudes. This knowledge can be a game-changer in our students' lives.

There are three types of people in this world: the optimist who sees the glass as half full, the pessimist who sees the glass as half empty, and the realist who sees 4.8 ounces of liquid in the glass and 7.2 ounces of air in the glass. I am most definitely a realist.

> Whether you think you can or you think you can't, you're right.
>
> —Henry Ford [1]

Ever since I started listening to positive speakers and turning off the news in the morning, my outlook changed dramatically. This can happen for your students as well. They just need some relevant instruction on how to do that.

✅ Key Takeaways

1. Our body will respond to "synthetic" emotions just the same as real ones.
2. Challenge students to surround themselves with people who will help them achieve their goals and maintain a positive attitude.
3. By understanding just some of the many influences that impact a student's attitude, we can begin to see the layers that make up a student's attitude.
4. Although it may be difficult, students can learn to control their attitudes.

💭 Points to Ponder—Chapter 14

1. Do you have a personal example of how your synthetic emotions made a situation worse?
2. What is a fun activity you can do with your students prior to a test to ensure they have the right attitude?

Reference

1. "Henry Ford: Quotable Quotes," *GoodReads*, https://www.good reads.com/quotes/978-whether-you-think-you-can-or-you-think-you-can-t--you-re, accessed August 20, 2021.

15

Pulse on Progress

Checking to See How They Have Improved and a Nice Dose of Credit

Pretend if you will, you have worked with your learners for months. They have defined success for themselves and even created a facets of success chart. So, you pose this Bowl Meeting question:

Bowl Meeting: Who Do You Think Is Successful?

You are primed and ready for thoughtful, beautiful answers, anticipating seeing a vast extent of growth in their thinking. However, with just one question, such excitement can come to a screeching halt. At least, if you receive some of the answers I did to this question. (Forgive the typos; these are direct quotes from eighth graders.)

DOI: 10.4324/9781003374497-15

- Jake: Elon Musk because he built many successful companies that make a lot of money.
- Lincoln: Mr. Beast, because he makes like sixty mill views per video and gets many sponsors and he has ads on his videos.
- Drake: jeff bezos because he has opened not only because he's the richest person but because he's opened some of the newest and advanced ideas to shipping.
- Aiden: steve jobs because he has the mutl billon dollar business.
- Kayley: Jeff bezos, I don't like him but hes rich.

Despite all our discussions and deep talks, they still couldn't get past connecting success to money. Society has really done a number on us all. Money can't be the sole definer of success. The answers students turned in prompted further discussion on how people can be successful in some facets of life but not all. I kept repeating, "Yes, that person is rich, but we have no idea about their personal life or how others treat them." A person might be successful in business, athletics, or Hollywood, but not enjoy success in other facets of their lives. This Bowl Meeting serves as a gauge and a glimpse into their minds, even after they have reflected so much. So, if you receive these kinds of answers, capitalize on it, and make this another teachable moment.

You can do that through another Bowl Meeting question:

Bowl Meeting: What Am I Becoming?

This question forces learners to take stock of the good, the bad, and the ugly about themselves. Being fully honest with oneself opens the doorway to self-improvement and personal growth. This correlates with a previous Bowl Question:

Bowl Meeting: What Attributes Do You Want Your Future Self to Have?

The important thing to remember is to pose these questions months apart.

This Bowl Meeting contains a preliminary question: What type of person do you want to be in ten years? Specifically, what personality traits or attributes do you want to have? It was very eye-opening how much more reflective they had become from the time I asked them about the attributes they want to have and the type of person they want to be ten years from now. Here is a list of some of the answers I have received, which serve as a heads-up on what you can expect.

- Leader
- Prioritize my work
- Mentally and emotionally stable
- Not perfect
- Not as self-conscious
- Approachable
- Less self-deprecating
- Less scared
- Confident
- Trustworthy

Each one of these examples provided a teachable moment. All of these came from asking them essentially the same question they had already been asked; it was just formulated slightly differently. I would like to point out the last trait in the examples I listed: trustworthy. Being trustworthy was the trait most commonly listed. Of course, I followed up with the question, "Are you not trustworthy now?" It was startling to hear student after student say they are trustworthy "most" of the time. It is amazing what comes out of these discussions! Essentially, asking the learners the same question months apart allows for a tremendous amount of reflection on their growth. If they recorded their initial response, that provides for an even deeper teachable moment.

Bowl Meeting: What Is a Credit Score? (No Bowl Used for This One.)

The next topic I want to review may seem like it has no connection to the previous discussion. Rest assured it is quite related, which is why I am such a strong believer in educating students about it. Sending them satisfactorily down the path to success must involve some discussion of finances. There is no way to address all the shortcomings the education system has right now in teaching students about finances, but one topic that can be discussed in a relatively short amount of time is a credit score. When looking at facets of success related to finances, you can add a great deal of value through just one short lesson on credit. Let me be transparent, I am by no means an expert on this topic. Nor do I want to be (mainly because it angers me).

Putting that aside, we need to discuss this topic with our learners. In my thirteen years of public school as a student, another four years of undergraduate studies, and two years of graduate work—plus countless other college courses—this topic did not arise even once! Plus, I spoke to a friend of mine who has a degree in finance and an MBA; not once did any of his classes discuss credit scores. I finally talked to someone who said at a private school in town, a session on credit scores is taught in senior year, in a remedial personal finance class. Are you kidding me? Every student needs to hear this, not just those struggling with math.

What follows is enough information to arm you for this discussion in your classroom. In sharing with you how I present this topic, I hope to convey why I am so passionate about it. Don't worry, I will give you a heads-up about the boring details. They are needed, though, so you can have a thorough discussion with your class—or, at a minimum—you can address some of the common questions you will field.

One reason this is so necessary is that teenagers start being inundated with credit card applications before they even graduate from high school. At the age of seventeen, I started getting credit card application forms in the mail. By age eighteen, they averaged four per day. This is no hyperbole; the bombardment of applications continued when I went off to college. Go to almost any campus today and you will see booths, tables, or tents set up with happy people offering free goodies for those who will sign up today. Seriously, what person doesn't want access to five hundred dollars for just signing their name on a piece of paper? Plus, a free t-shirt? That is a good day! Or is it?

Taking a Free Ride

What proceeds is the story of two brothers (not by blood, but by bond). Both students were of above-average intelligence, hailed from lower middle-class families, and stormed the castle of college together. Neither one had ever received any training on credit. Let's call one of the students Dwight, and the other Creed. As they excitedly hit the campus, they felt the rush of power and freedom. Their first opportunity to flex said freedom occurred when a rather nice-looking girl suggested affixing their signatures to an application for their first credit card. They didn't hesitate!

At this point, their joyride began. They both started spending at a relatively equal pace. Dwight and Creed shopped for clothes, ate out, and bought a bunch of frivolous trinkets. You know, the usual "stuff." Creed especially loved it. Instead of doing laundry, he just bought more clothes. Need dinner? Why not charge dinner at Outback Steakhouse once or twice a week? What college student doesn't need a good steak now and then?

Dwight went along for the ride ... for a while. But as time progressed, he started feeling uneasy about the amount of debt he was piling up. Creed, however, went full steam ahead. When one card was full, he would just open another, paying off credit cards with credit cards. Then Creed started gambling online—naturally, on a credit card. All the while, Dwight sensed something was wrong with such wasteful spending. In addition, Dwight's disdain for owing anyone anything festered, although his willpower would soon face a sharp test.

"Yes, I Will Take the Samurai Swords, Please."

While visiting his sister, Amy, in Tampa, Dwight took a trip to the mall. There he saw the ultimate prize: three samurai swords, gleaming under fluorescent bulbs and displayed in breathtaking fashion. Since childhood, Dwight had secretly wanted to own a samurai sword. On top of that, they were only three hundred bucks. What a deal! He could just take out his card and swipe away to become the proud owner of not one, not two, but *three* samuraI swords. Dwight's emotional brain screamed, "Hi-yah!" But his logical brain countered with: "Hi-nah!" The battle raged as Dwight revisited those swords three times before leaving the mall empty-handed. After careful and extended deliberation, "Hi-nah" won out and a new man emerged without samuraI swords (and woefully unprepared should he suddenly get attacked by any samurai-bearing ninjas).

Prior to this time, Dwight never missed a credit card payment. This increased his credit rating and by graduation his credit limit for the one card he used all the time had surpassed ten thousand dollars. Although his credit was intact, his credit card debt at graduation was more than twelve hundred dollars.

It took Creed much longer to listen to his "Hi-nah" instead of his "Hi-yah." Before he finished school, Credit had racked up more than nine thousand dollars in credit card debt, along with a dismal credit score.

Making Wise Choices

I present this story to my students every year on the next-to-last day of school. The only change I make is substituting two of my current students' names into the story. I stress to them that this lesson is probably the most important one I will ever teach them. Most likely, they will never get it again. With added embellishment, I walk them through the start of two students' credit life as I just mentioned.

Student A makes all the right choices. She has a higher credit score as time progresses. This allows her to get a good job, buy a car, rent an apartment, and eventually buy a good home. Student B makes bad credit decisions: overspends, misses payments, pays a higher interest rate, can't live where he wants, can't buy a home, and winds up getting kicked out of a buddy's house and living in a van with Jackson ... bankrupt. I parallel each step of the way and each decision they make on the board for them.

Like I said, since I embellish the story, I just scratch it out on the board. I rarely write on the board, so it is a change for them as well. This also allows me to freestyle as I go. The information in Table 15.1 is what I have displayed on my smartboard (I will give those details shortly).

TABLE 15.1
Information displayed during discussion of credit.

Credit Score	
How do they get a credit score? 1. Three Companies gather the data. 2. Equifax, Experian, Transunion. 3. FICO, a separate company, then interprets the data and assigns a score.	**What is a credit score range?** For FICO, it is 300–850 **What do they look at?** 1. Payment History (35%) 2. Amount Owed (30%) 3. Length of Credit History (15%) 4. New Credit (10%) 5. Type of Credit Used (10%)

The following is an outline of the essentials of this lesson. It is extremely abbreviated. You are smart. You can fill in any gaps with your strong teaching ability. Plus, add some personal anecdotes.

1. Frame this well. I tell them this is the most important lesson I will teach them because it is most likely the only time they will hear it.
2. Introduce to them Social Security numbers and that when anyone wants you to write it down, they can impact your credit.
3. What is credit? What is a credit score? What is interest?
4. How do they get a credit score? Three companies gather the data: Equifax, Experian, and TransUnion. FICO, a separate company, then interprets the data and assigns a score. It is a bit more involved, but this sums it up [1].
5. What is a credit score's range? For FICO, it is 300–850 [2].
6. What do they look at?
   a. payment history (35%).
   b. amount owed (30%).
   c. length of credit history (15%).
   d. new credit (10%).
   e. type of credit used (10%).

7. Make up one heck of a story comparing two of your students, as I described above. Parallel each step of the way. Take them through multiple ups and downs on their credit journey.
8. Give them hope. Explain how, if they handle the credit score well, they can use it to their benefit, like qualifying for cash back cards and lower interest rates.
9. Go over the number one rule about spending. (See next section)

After I cover the nuts and bolts, I discuss with them my big rule and the things worth using credit to buy. I tell them bluntly: this might be different than what their parents believe. But by giving them multiple sides to a discussion, students can formulate their own route to follow.

Never Spend Money You Don't Have

You don't *really need* a samural sword. If you can't live without it, then save up and buy it outright. What is wrong with waiting to make a purchase? Use your credit to your advantage. If you must make that purchase, then put it on the credit card and pay it off at the end of the month. Let your credit card company PAY YOU for using their card. Plenty advertise cash back rewards, but the only way you can get those cards is if you have good credit. That's why I regularly repeat this rule: "Never spend money you don't have." After reminding them they don't need a samural sword, I discuss the two (and a half) things I think are worthy of going into debt to purchase: an education, a house, and—maybe—a car. Each is reviewed as follows.

Regarding going in debt for a college education, one study by Georgetown University and the Pew Research Center says college grads make more than a million dollars more over their career than a person with only a high school diploma [3]. In choosing their college, they need to make that decision based on their financial support, not on their emotional draw to become a (Florida) Gator or a (Miami) Hurricane.

More often than not, the training for a career occurs on the job; that diploma just gets them in the door. Therefore, a person seeking a degree in education or social work, might not want to go to a high cost, Ivy League-type school and walk out of school with tens of thousands of dollars of debt. When I finished college at the University of Central Florida, I had twelve thousand dollars in student loans. A former coworker, on the other hand, wasn't so lucky. He went to a private college and racked up over forty thousand dollars in student loans. (How do you say "ouch" in Spanish?)

According to the chipper folks at Debt.org, in 2017 students had an average student loan debt of $37,172 [4].

Are you convinced yet why we need to talk to our students about credit cards and spending? Do you see the connection with this lesson to success? There are a lot of options out there to help students pay for college or further education. They just have to pay attention and seek them out. Let's take ownership of students' success and not just our particular subject area. That way, they can start making informed decisions that better their lives.

When it comes to buying a home, most people will have to go into debt to make that purchase. Most of the time it will pay off as they build equity in the home. As long as the timing is right (meaning the market is a good time to buy) and they are not overspending, then a home can be worth going into debt to purchase.

On the other hand, a car does not gain equity. (Yes, you will need to explain the definition of equity.) It depreciates in value the minute you drive it off the lot. According to the folks at Carfax, a car's value can depreciate more than 20% in value over the first year of ownership, followed by 10% per year for each of the next four years [5].

That is why I stress a car can be worth flexing their credit muscles, but only if it is a smart purchase. Once again, though, one that they make with their financial mind on the wheel and their emotional mind steering them down debt lane.

What Happened to Dwight and Creed?

It is time to confess my motivation behind this lesson and the story of Dwight and Creed. I am/was Dwight. I hate owing anyone anything. Within the first two years of graduating from college, I paid off that twelve hundred bucks on my credit card and haven't paid a dime in interest since. While I was paying that debt off, they kept expanding my credit limit; it reached twenty-five thousand dollars on that card. That is ridiculous, especially considering at the time I only made twenty-four thousand dollars a year. Still, my hard work paid off. The credit card companies are paying me to use their cards! (I feel special.)

As of the time of writing this, the only debt I have is my mortgage. I have a goal of paying it off in ten years, if not sooner. I did get some instruction about credit along the way, so I can't take all the credit. Starting in college, my aunt and uncle constantly planted seeds in my mind about the importance of credit. They happen to be the only people I know with a perfect 850! And by the way, no, I never did buy any samural swords.

Creed was my good friend, Sean. We met in fourth grade and were roommates in college. He met a wonderful woman, Angela, along the way. She helped turn him around. He is now an extremely successful financial planner with an amazing business helping people succeed in their life planning. He used some of those early lessons as catalysts to catapult him to great financial success. Without a doubt, I am super proud of him!

I convey the example of Sean and me, along with other content, in one class period. Sounds like a lot, but I have been presenting it this way for years. I realize some of what I have shared may differ from some of your personal beliefs, but what is the harm in teaching students to only buy things they can afford and be aware of the good and bad sides of credit? Again, let's arm them with the knowledge, then they can make their own decisions when the time comes.

I absolutely share the outcomes about Sean and myself with my students. Not to brag, but to give them an understanding that *this can be done.* I emphasize that Sean's circumstances in overcoming such debt and credit challenges is an anomaly. Most people do not come out of that situation so well, but it is important for them to learn that, even if they make mistakes, they can dig their way out. Remember, they don't need samuraI swords!

Make teaching about credit and spending your own. Share your own personal stories that you have a strong emotional connection to as well. The students will feel that and connect with the lesson even more, as illustrated by Figure 15.1.

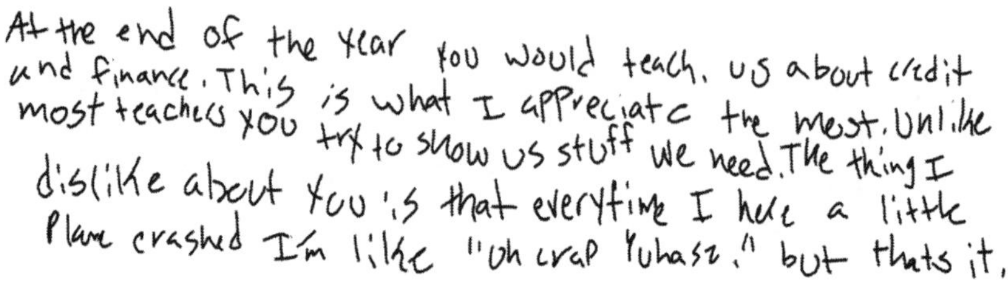

At the end of the year you would teach. us about credit and finance. This is what I appreciate the most. Unlike most teachers you try to show us stuff we need. The thing I dislike about you is that everytime I hee a little plan crashed I'm like "oh crap I'uhasz." but thats it,

FIGURE 15.1 This student is grateful for a lesson on credit.

The Truth About Credit

The first time I presented this information to my class, a young girl raised her hand and asked, "Is it bad if my parents use my name on the electric bill?" My heart dropped. She had barely begun her life and her parents were already making a mess of her credit like they had their own. I responded, "That's up to the circumstances" although inside I was screaming, "YES! They are messing you up!" I always encourage students to ask their parents about credit. This way the conversation will get started early.

One time a student returned the next day and said when she asked her parents about credit because I told her to, they responded, "It's none of your business." Obviously, there was a disconnect. I didn't want to know anything about their personal business, but I do want parents (and teachers) to talk to their kids about it. It's not a leap to imagine there had been some mistakes with credit. Yet, why don't parents discuss their mistakes with their kids so they don't perpetuate the cycle? I not only don't get it; it also ticks me off. That emphasizes even more how we as educators have to step up and have this discussion with learners.

We want them to have the most successful and fulfilled life they can. A good credit score gives you leverage. A bad one closes doors in your life that you truly wish were open.

> Then there's the Social Security Administration. They tell us, "Your nine-digit social security number is the first and continuous connection with Social Security. It helps us identify and accurately record your covered wages or self-employment earnings [6]." But it isn't just Uncle Sam who's paying attention to those earnings. Credit agencies often use social security numbers to identify your account and learn more about you.

So how are Americans doing handling their credit? Not too well. Look at some examples:

- According to a *USA Today* article, in 2019 Americans owed on average over six thousand dollars on their credit cards [7]. If you are a teacher reading this, that is a lot of school days you would work to pay that off! On top of that, in July 2021, the average credit score was 711, which is only "good" (the higher rankings are "very good" and "exceptional") [8].
- Better watch your back ... ground check. Based on a survey conducted by the National Association of Professional Background Screeners, more than 30% of companies run a credit check on some of their candidates. Sixteen percent check all their candidates [9].
- Straight from the snaggletooth horse's mouth: Guess what can happen from just one late payment? If you have a higher credit score, ONE late payment of 30 days can samurai-sword-slice your score by 90 to 110 points! [10]

Are you kidding me with that last one? On top of that, if you close a current, up-to-date account with no balance, it can hurt you. Prior to buying my house, I wanted to make sure everything was polished and pearly white with my credit score, so

I closed an account I hadn't used in years. It dropped my score from 833 to 785. I still haven't been able to get it back up to 833 (in case you can't tell, this really irritates me).

Stung by Information

When I was a young kid, I was stomping through the hills of West Virginia with my sister, Grace, and two friends. We walked in a single-file line, led by the other boy, and followed by his sister, my sister, and me as the caboose. The next thing you know, the line leader started dancing around and screaming. Then, his sister started yelping and hopping around too. Next my sister shrieked. I didn't know what was going on, but I knew I wanted no part of it. Taking a wide berth around the spot they just walked, I could see the three of them tearing down that mountain. My sister turned back and yelled, "Grab my headband!"

Stupid mistake. I turned around to look for her dumb headband, which is when I discovered why they were all squealing: yellow jackets! One landed on my knee and stung the mess out of me. Dropping her headband, I tore down that mountain like the rest of them. (I am certain she still hasn't forgiven me for dropping it.) What we didn't know was that lurking in the ground up there on that mountain was a yellow jacket nest. My friend got stung three times, his sister nineteen, and Grace more than twenty. Me? Just once (hey, my knee really hurt). The folks we were staying with said they heard us whooping and hollering all the way down the hill. Then, they were kind enough to share: "Oh yeah, there's a yellow jacket's nest in the ground up there."

That was some information we could have used YESTERDAY! Credit is the exact same way. People know about it, but don't bother sharing the information until it is too late. Poor credit can be like a swarm of yellow jackets. If you don't know about them, they can sting you before you are even aware of their presence. But it does not have to be that way. It takes educating students on the pros and cons of credit to keep them from getting stung. Why not share this information with them? They will literally thank you for it.

What evidence do I have? Don't take my word for it. Below, and in Figures 15.2 and 15.3 are some unsolicited quotes from a parent and several students.

Your advice about staying out of debt springs to mind as an example of really excellent advice you've shared with your students over the years. She brings home your nuggets of wisdom to share with us, and it's impactful for kids to hear to hear these things from other adults they respect, and not just parents (who are full of advice constantly!)

—Jennifer C.

Are you convinced yet of the need to implement these topics in your classroom? If you are still reading this, that is a good sign.

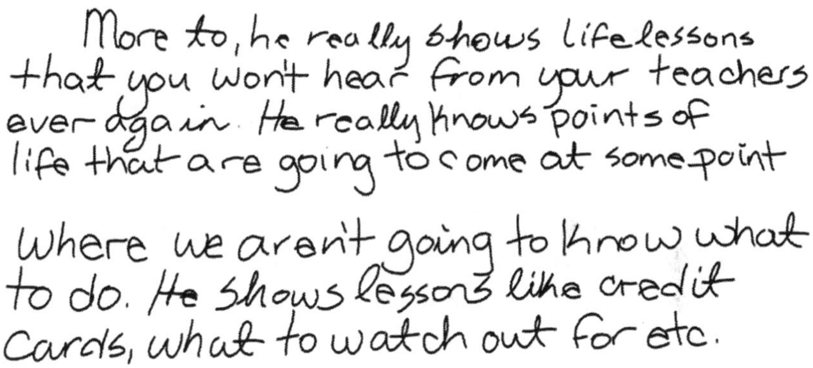

More to, he really shows Life lessons that you won't hear from your teachers ever again. He really knows points of life that are going to come at some point

Where we aren't going to know what to do. He shows lessons like credit cards, what to watch out for etc.

FIGURE 15.2 Another student showing gratitude for being taught about credit.

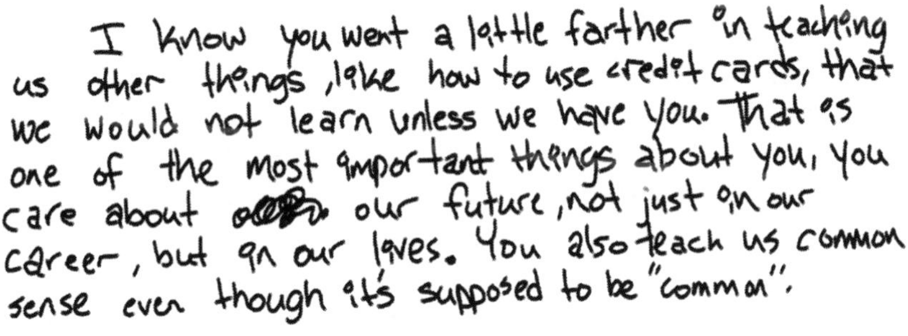

I know you went a little farther in teaching us other things, like how to use credit cards, that we would not learn unless we have you. That is one of the most important things about you, you care about our future, not just on our career, but on our lives. You also teach us common sense even though it's supposed to be "common".

FIGURE 15.3 This student really appreciated the life connection in class.

If you discuss this cold turkey, it might be a bit of adjustment for you and your students. The best way to teach the topics outlined in this book is through established class meetings. Move them from their typical seats so they understand the importance of the topic you are about to discuss. This breaks up the monotony of everyday experience. Plus, there are many other reasons to have a well-established classroom meeting routine.

Have you ever listened to a pair of middle schoolers talking to each other? They talk over each other about two different topics while constantly interrupting one another. It can get a bit mind numbing! Classroom meetings allow students to practice their listening skills. Let's face it; most people are terrible listeners. Try this, or maybe you have already experienced it. Complain to an adult about a $275 speeding ticket you JUST got on the way to work. Act real upset about it. Now, see how long it takes for that person to tell you about the ticket they got in the past. (Or brag how they never got one.) You don't care about years ago. You are feeling the pain NOW! Were they listening to you? Not one bit.

Teaching Listening

Classroom meetings are so important. You are teaching them how to listen. The students are reminded to listen and not react, even if they want to. First, they need to listen. Then, they can be heard. The student who is sharing her passion is to be listened to and not get stepped on by another student who shares the same passion but cares little about what their classmate is saying. I always remind students that this is a time to listen, because good communication begins with listening.

Classroom meetings cultivate a climate of trust. Think back to the example I gave you of the student who said his success was contingent on his father's approval. When pulled aside by our counselor, the student did not want to talk about it. Classroom meetings where all students are sharing can break down walls and allow students to be vulnerable. On many occasions, students have cried and even confessed things they probably shouldn't have. Students frequently break down over relatives or other loved ones who have died. They might not always have the words to say, but at the end of the day, they know their voice was heard.

This brings me to my next point: often, educators do not take the time to really listen to their students. (Please understand when I say "educators" I am lumping myself in that category.) It is tough. There are so many external demands on you in the classroom and now that our evaluation is tied to student gains, we have less time than ever to listen to our students. Classroom meetings force you to take the time to listen. *They empower the students with a voice!* Students just want to be heard.

My buy-in to classroom meetings didn't truly occur until I was teaching in a Title I school. These kids came from the inner city and did not care one whit about physical science. Plus, my school was early in its transitioning to a magnet school, which refers to a school offering a specialized curriculum to students outside its normal attendance boundaries—and which is capable of attracting students from differing social, economic, ethnic, and racial backgrounds. By their own admission, my students felt that all the teachers cared about was getting rid of them so we could have a nice "white" magnet school. (Of course, I didn't get that nugget of information until AFTER I started my classroom meetings.)

Not surprisingly, there was terrible behavior in the hallways, which led to poor behavior in the classroom. Bright students did not give one bit of effort toward my subject area. Finally, I had had enough. One day, I had them all come sit in a circle and we started talking. At that point, I just wanted to vent, but it slowly turned into me asking them questions about annoying hallway behavior. I didn't just ask, though; I also sincerely listened. It was like something strange happened. They all shared the same gripes and complaints; airing them *created a bond within my classroom.*

Thus, the genesis of Bowl Meetings. On several occasions, students said I was the only teacher who ever listened to them. Some of them even wanted me to move up to teaching high school so I could keep on being their science teacher! (To be transparent, I thought some of them couldn't stand me.) I continued to teach my subject area, but I realized these students needed a way bigger lesson.

> They needed to learn teachers do care.

They needed to get that we care more about their life success than the short-term success in our classroom. *They needed to be heard.* Once learners get that message, they will start working harder in your subject area.

There are plenty of books and articles out there regarding classroom meetings, which you can peruse if you need more details. My whole reason to mention this as a topic is, if you buy into the idea of classroom meetings, then hopefully you will see the benefits in discussing the main topics I am presenting. If we do not make a conscious effort to think about thinking, and a conscious effort to discuss and educate our students about the topics I am reviewing, we are not only doing a disservice to our students but to our nation as a whole. Just in case you are still on the fence about taking class time to have these discussions, Figure 15.4 is one more "convincer."

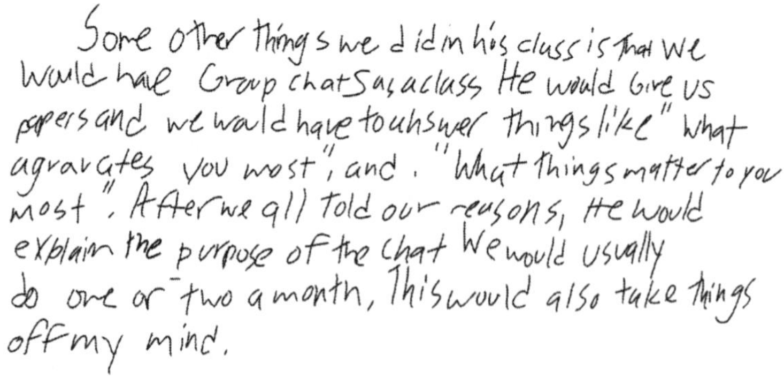

Some other things we did in his class is that we would have Group chats as a class He would give us papers and we would have to answer things like "what agravates you most", and "What things matter to you most". After we all told our reasons, He would explain the purpose of the chat We would usually do one or two a month, This would also take things off my mind.

FIGURE 15.4 These class "meetings" helped ease this student's mind.

✓ Key Takeaways

1. Your lesson on credit might be the only time a student is taught about the subject.

2. Credit companies start preying on students as young as 16 years old.
3. Well-structured class meetings teach the students better listening skills.

🗨 Points to Ponder—Chapter 15

1. What's your personal credit story?
2. Did anyone teach you about credit?
3. What other ways can you teach your students better listening skills?

References

1. Louis DeNicola, "How Is Your Credit Score Determined?", *Experian*, February 12, 2021, https://www.experian.com/blogs/ask-experian/how-is-your-credit-score-determined/
2. Jim Akin, "What Are the Different Credit Score Ranges?", *Experian*, June 23, 2020, https://www.experian.com/blogs/ask-experian/infographic-what-are-the-different-scoring-ranges/
3. Coastline Staff, "Why College Grads Earn A Million More Than Those Who Don't Go," *Coastline College*, September 26, 2019, https://blog.coastline.edu/why-college-grads-earn-a-million-more-than-those-who-dont-go-2
4. "Students & Debt," *Debt.org*, https://www.debt.org/students/, accessed August 23, 2021.
5. Rick Popely, "Car Depreciation: How Much It Costs You," *Carfax*, February 3, 2021, https://www.carfax.com/blog/car-depreciation
6. "Social Security Number and Card," *SocialSecurityAdministration.gov*, https://www.ssa.gov/ssnumber/, accessed August 23, 2021.
7. Samuel Stebbbins, "Where Credit Card Debt Is the Worst in the US: States with the Highest Average Balances," *USA Today*, March 7, 2019 (updated April 26, 2019), https://www.usatoday.com/story/money/personalfinance/2019/03/07/credit-card-debt-where-average-balance-highest-across-us/39129001/
8. Gerrl Detweiler, "What Is the Average Credit Score?" *Credit.com*, July 28, 2021, https://www.credit.com/credit-scores/what-is-the-average-credit-score/

9. Susan Ladika, "Employer Credit Checks: Who Does Them, How They Work and What Laws Apply," *Creditcards.com*, July 15, 2019, https://www.creditcards.com/credit-card-news/employer-job-credit-report-check-1270/

10. "How Might My Actions Affect Credit Scores?" *Equifax Knowledge Center*, https://www.equifax.com/personal/education/credit/score/how-do-your-actions-affect-your-credit-scores/, accessed August 23, 2021.

16

Executing the Plan

Realistically Putting All This in Motion

What comes next? You must be willing to let go of some class time teaching your subject area. Realistically, if all you do is give up four class periods in a school year, you can convey the bare bones of what I wish for every student to hear. Here are some examples of days you can choose: (1) days that are already tattered by standardized testing; (2) the first week of school as a way to get to know them; and (3) days that fall right before a long break. I choose days when I feel my class has been slapped in the face long enough with my subject matter and I am seeking to re-establish a stronger bond with them. As I mentioned, I teach my credit topic on the next-to-last day of the school year.

Before closing, it is necessary to leave you with an outline of how to implement these lessons. At the end of this book, in the appendices, I have included a number of resources you can use to teach them. But, if you want a simplistic way of teaching them without even making a copy of a worksheet, here is a suggestion. If your students use composition notebooks, have them record your discussion information, starting on the last page and working forward—mainly to keep these life lessons separate from material on your subject. It is vital that students visually see and track their ideas and responses. They need to revisit and modify them.

DOI: 10.4324/9781003374497-16

Now, if you give a lot of notes, this method will not work for you, but I am guessing most students do not fill up their notebooks all the way to the end. Everything listed below will be written down by your students and revisited later. The perfect scenario is to weave these topics in periodically, even if it is just a few minutes at the end of a class. Repetition is the key. Even though I list them as "Day 1," "Day 2," and so on, many of these lessons require further discussion and emphasis. In Appendix H, you will find a simple checklist I use to keep track of which class has been taught what concept. a,. This list reflects the *bare minimum*. Now, to the outline.

1. Day 1 and 2: What are you passionate about? How can you turn your passion into a career? Have students research what education is needed, pay scale, what people they could contact who are already working in that field, and so on.
2. Day 3: How do you define success? Really dive into this one and teach them "Facets of Success."
3. Day 4: What motivates you? Give them examples.
4. Day 5: Teach goal setting and goal writing. Establish an outward demonstration and compilation of goals, like the footprint example in Chapter 9. It needs to be something they can track. If nothing else, have students write them down.
5. Day 6: Attitude. Describe ways to change their attitudes. This is an ongoing lesson that you should weave throughout all instruction.
6. Day 7: Revisit goals. Evaluate how they are doing while setting new ones. This could be done in just a few minutes, so it might not take a class period. Do this periodically.
7. Day 8: Credit score.

Making a Diary

Through this process, I keep track of which class has received what content by using the checklist previously mentioned in

Appendix H. Also, after I teach about goal setting, I have the students begin a video diary addressing the content we have discussed so far. They answer the following in their diary. This is the information I have displayed for my students.

Video Time Capsule

Your video capsule is a conversation you are going to have with your future self. Please include the following:

1. Today's Date
2. What are you passionate about? How are going to turn that into a career?
3. Describe three facets of success and three goals for each of those facets. 1-year goals, 5-year goals and 10-year goals
4. Describe what motivates you.
5. Describe two ways you can add "VALUE" to yourself over the next year.
6. Describe in detail the current goal you have written down. (From our lesson on goals.)

By now your mind is screaming, "Are you kidding me, give up almost two weeks of class!" Yes. Yes. And yes. But let's reprogram that mind of yours. View it as one class period a month. You will not be giving up two weeks of class. You will be giving them invaluable information that few other teachers will ever take the time to teach them. You are giving them information that will allow them to make the best decisions they can when they graduate.

I guarantee you when they become adults, they will not remember that test you are working so hard to prepare them for, but they will remember the life lessons you taught them. Again, what do want to build, an army of students successful in a subject area, or an army of successful students...period? Ease your way into it. Try teaching just one lesson—just one—and see how it is received. If it falls flat, you can scrap the whole idea. But I guarantee you, your students will embrace it.

Valuable Topics

School districts are beginning to recognize the value of spending class time discussing many of the topics shared in this book. In 2020, my school district took a huge step in looking at the success of the whole student and not just their success in academic studies. This is an exciting time for our students because the door has been opened for teachers to formally teach about some of the social and emotional learning (SEL) competencies (in business, these are often called "soft skills"). They are as follows:

1. Self-awareness
2. Self-management
3. Social awareness
4. Relationship skills
5. Responsible decision-making [1].

Having students outline their definitions of emotional success means they have already begun their journey in learning these SEL goals. Also, armed with the understanding of the influences on their attitudes and how to maintain a healthy attitude, students are ready to take on many of the emotional challenges that will flare up on their way.

Weaving the lessons of this book into your classroom, you will make tremendous strides in accomplishing the SEL competencies involving self-awareness and self-management. Some of the key components of those two areas involve identifying emotions, recognizing strengths, self-confidence, impulse control, stress management, self-discipline, self-motivation, and goal setting. The great thing is the lessons captured in this book give you an easy way of addressing those crucial elements.

Look at the first competency of self-awareness. The only way you, your students, or anyone else can undergo legitimate, life-changing, and long-lasting self-improvement is by braving the refining fires of self-reflection. Self-awareness can only occur through deep reflection.

Retiring the Retreads

At this point, you might be overwhelmed by the information conveyed in this book and the request I am making to you. Rest assured, if you begin to integrate this content little by little, it will not be that bad. In fact, it will be quite enjoyable. My purpose in providing so much information for you is to give you enough background, reflection, and courage to teach these concepts. The good thing is you can use as little or as much of this information as you want: it is up to you. However, the more content of this book you can implement in your classroom, the better chance your students will have at obtaining their definitions of success. It will just take a small change in your classroom routine to make a large change for your students. Plus, you will be amazed how much you can learn about your students from this process.

Much of my adult life I clung to regret like a life preserver. All the while, I didn't realize how clinging to that life preserver hindered me from swimming to the lifeboat. I didn't understand the lessons in this book. To be blunt, I wasn't taught the lessons in this book; I had to learn the hard way. The hard way meant being enslaved in a dungeon built by my poor attitude and regret.

Our students don't have to live that way. This journey began with me wishing to change the direction of my students' lives and empowering them with this knowledge to live much happier, success-filled lives. It has mutated to a point where I wish to impact more students than those who step into the confines of my classroom. I want to impact millions of students. This is my driving passion, motivation, and definition of success, all rolled into one.

Educators have a choice. They can complain about the state of our educational system, or they can change it. The only person you can change in your life is yourself. You are truly the most important person anyway. You CAN change you. You CAN change your outlook on education and use your influence to redirect and reshape your students. The voids in education will always be there, so let's improve the condition of education by first improving ourselves. Then, we can share this knowledge with our students. Learning the messages in this book and then sharing them with our students begins to help fill those voids. There are plenty of great subjects taught in school, but we are neglecting more pertinent, life-changing topics.

If we can recalibrate our students to think about thinking by deeply reflecting on the right questions, they will find a higher value and meaning in education. Once they define success, embrace goal setting, and put it into practice, they can map out their future. By learning how to monitor and regulate their attitudes, they are ready for whatever storms life may bring on their way. Having an early understanding of credit scores will help them avoid a major financial downfall and help them to achieve monetary success. Judging by the abysmal picture of credit card debt and credit scores, too many adults didn't learn about this before it was too late.

It is time to start being proactive. To start a wave of change, we do not need approval from Congress, the board of education, our principal, the garbage man, or the old lady next door. We need to stop the wheels of education from spinning in place and put some tread back on those tires. Or better yet, let's change those tires altogether. A great quote I once heard stated, "People will work hard at their job, but not at their future." If you tinker with the wording just a smidge, the quote takes on a whole new life for teachers.

> Students will work hard in school, but not at planning their future.

People can remain very busy without being very effective. This relates directly to our students. Often, students will go to great lengths to *prepare for the future,* but little of that effort is used to *plan their future.* Let's put education back into the hands of educators, change our students' futures, and start ensuring the efficacy of education. Our students not only want the information presented in this book; they need it—even though they don't know it yet. However, once they realize it, they not only embrace it, but cheer for it. I am not lying to you. When my students discover we are doing a class discussion, they literally cheer! Let's spur them on to successful lives. Success in any field takes discipline, perseverance, and conviction. The success of these lessons in your classroom requires the same. However, the rewards of these lessons are beyond measure.

Please understand all the words in this book originate from a humble, yet confident standpoint. I wish this book to be a resource, not just read through and tossed aside. I hope it is something that is picked up and referenced throughout your journey of creating wildly successful students. There are amazing teachers out there who do amazing things. There are teachers who can take this information and present it in ways that I could never imagine. It really takes teaching something to thoroughly learn it. That is how I feel about the content of this book. It has to be taught to be truly learned. Trust me, I am STILL learning this content. All I have done is make observations about ideas that have worked well in my classroom and shared them with you.

Final Thoughts

In a way, I have misled you from the beginning. This book is not about success. The very word implies a final destination or stopping point. Success is by no means a destination. This book is about balancing successes to find fulfillment. Even fulfillment is not a destination. It is an ongoing journey, a search, and a restless inquiry. The only thing required to start that journey is a growth mindset.

As you undoubtedly have encountered in life, not many people embrace a growth mindset. When you do meet someone who does, you will recognize it right away. They will possess an insatiable appetite to learn. But not just to learn—exuding a burning desire to improve in all things, they put forth the effort to do so. I hope I have instilled in you the outlook toward changing yourself into a growth mindset and putting this same outlook into learners.

As I hope you have discerned, it is not one simple step, but a series of steps leading to life-improving changes. It is asking the right questions to begin the journey. And, by revisiting those same questions along the journey, empowering the learners to stay the course. Life has a way of being merciless at times, but then again, it can be so giving and kind as well. It is through those light and dark moments that our resolve gets tested. During those times is when the right questions need to be asked again. Whether it is: "How can I maintain these great things?" or "What must I do to move out of these trials?" the right questions revolve around understanding yourself.

I know I'm repeating myself here, but it's worth one more reminder: *There is no way to have authentic, life-changing, long-lasting self-improving change without first enduring a soul-searching, gut-wrenching self-reflection.* At this point, I would like to modify that ever so slightly: There is no way to have authentic, life-changing, long-lasting, self-improving change without CONTINUALLY enduring a soul-searching, gut-wrenching self-reflection. You have to continually strip back the layers of emotions and traumas as you have faced years (maybe even decades) of the wrong inner voice haunting you. Once that occurs, then you can continually carve out and live a life of fulfillment.

This book is my way of saying, "I wish I would have known this when I was younger." Then why don't we teach our learners the things we wish we would have known, so they can avoid some of the pitfalls we suffered? Asking the right questions doesn't mean life will be without trials or tribulations. However, understanding how to ask the right questions can help a person endure and overcome those challenges.

Now, I present to you my call to action. We all know education is lacking in some ways, but overly focusing on that aspect will defeat everything this book stands for. I outlined that information at the opening of this book as a way for you to be reflective. We cannot get stuck in reflection, agonizing, regretting, and whining our way to inaction. *Reflection allows us to unravel the past. Action and execution propel us to unlocking the future.* We must be forward thinkers. Through asking the right questions, we have begun to "think" for the first time. By "thinking" for the first time, we have begun to evolve education. That is the reflection part. For a full evolution, we need the action and execution part. Neither of those two things can happen without you. Without you, there can be no evolution. Without you, there can be no "thinking" for the first time. Without you, there can be no growth mindset.

If for any reason you are still on the fence, I challenge you to take just one of these ideas to your learners. Find the one concept you can present to students with the most earnest heart. Find the one concept that resonates deeply with you and share it with your learners. Don't just connect with that idea, let your learners see and hear how you connect with it. Personalize it. I guarantee you once you connect with an idea and then you connect that idea with your learner, you will both be hooked. You will see how great an impact you are making on your learner (see Figures 16.1 and 16.2). Your learner will share in the eye-opening experience. Or I should say "mind-opening" experience. That will just be the beginning, but it will be a very exciting beginning, one that leads to a huge leap in thinking and the genesis of a fulfilled life. Your learners will ask to be enlightened more. And it all started with you asking them the right questions.

> Also, you taught us lessons like not not being a scrounge. The activity where we circle up and talk about different subjects has also helped me tremendously. It make me think about what I should be doing with my life what I am hoping to accomplish with what I do. To me, that is more valuable than any STEM education.

FIGURE 16.1 Just an added "convincer" to teach this content.

> Here are just a few lessons I've learned from your class:
> 1) Put real effort into everything you do. Don't just wing it.
> 2) Never settle for a first draft. You can always improve.
> 3) Really understand the things you learn, don't just memorize them.
> 4) Save early, save often.
> 5) Be passionate in all you do.
> 6) Identify your goals and figure out how to get on the right path.
> 7) Never, ever go into debt unless you need to for a house, an education, or maybe a car.

FIGURE 16.2 I could not have paid this student for a better summation of the school year!

☑ Key Takeaways

1. If we can recalibrate our students to think about thinking by deeply reflecting on the right questions, they will find a higher value and meaning in education.
2. You will be giving them invaluable information that few other teachers will ever take the time to teach them.
3. You are giving them information that will allow them to make the best decisions they can when they graduate.
4. There is no way to have authentic, life-changing, long-lasting self-improving change without first enduring a soul-searching, gut-wrenching self-reflection.

Reference

1. "Core Topics," *Social Emotional Learning (SEL) Tools*, https://mylearning tools.org/core-topics-summary/, accessed August 25, 2021.

Appendix A

Bowl Meetings and Careers

Topics you can use for the classroom discussions (Bowl Meetings).

- What are you passionate about and how can you turn that into a career?
- What attributes do you want your future self to have?
- Name three attributes you like about yourself.
- What do you worry about the most?
- What is your definition of success?
- What value do you bring to the table?
- What does sacrifice mean to you?
- What does self-discipline mean to you?
- What motivates you in life and school?
- What are you doing to be emotionally successful?
- What superlatives are you?
- What is a goal you can obtain in the next three months?
- Name two personality traits that annoy you.
- How do you handle negative feedback on social media?
- How have you failed in the last week? The last month?
- Tell us about a time when you were really embarrassed.
- What fears do you have that would stop you from achieving your success?
- Describe a time when you had a really bad attitude about doing something, but once you did it, it turned out okay.
- List three things you are grateful for.
- Name two things you are successful at right now.
- Name two things about yourself that make you special or unique.
- Who do you think is successful?
- What am I becoming?
- What attributes do you want your future self to have?
- What is a credit score? (No bowl used for this one.)

- ◆ Write down a message of no more than ten words that you would tell yourself of five years ago (it doesn't have to be a full sentence).
- ◆ Name two annoying traits you find in people.
- ◆ If you could change two things about this school, what would they be?
- ◆ What is a personal motto or quote you live by?
- ◆ What role does television play in your life and the life of your family?
- ◆ What are you most afraid of?
- ◆ Name two things about yourself that I don't know.
- ◆ If your house caught fire and you had time to grab three things, what would they be? (Exclude people and pets.)
- ◆ Describe a time when someone surprised you with kindness.
- ◆ What kind thing can you do for someone this weekend? (Might have to think about this one.)

Appendix B

Rapid-Fire Questions and Suggested Timeline of Implementation

Rapid-Fire Questions

1. What are you really good at doing?
2. What is something you enjoy?
3. What is something your friends and family say you are good at doing?
4. Observing what you are good at and what you enjoy, is there any way to use those things in the service of others?
5. In your eyes, what is wrong with the world?
6. What are you bad at doing but wish you were better? What are you bad at doing and *know* you need to be better at? What do your family and friends say you are bad at doing?
7. What are you dying to get better at or learn?
8. What is something that comes very easy to you?
9. What is something you could teach someone else … really well?
10. What is something you could talk about for three hours straight?
11. What skills do you possess that others don't?
12. What makes you feel proud you accomplished?

Quick Glance at the Most Essential Lessons

1. Days 1 and 2: What are you passionate about? How can you turn your passion
into a career? Have students research what education is needed, pay scale, what people they could contact who are already working in that field, and so forth.
2. Day 3: How do you define success? Really dive into this one and teach them "Facets of Success."
3. Day 4: What motivates you? Give them examples.
4. Day 5: Teach goal setting and goal writing. Establish an outward demonstration and compilation of goals, like the footprint example in Chapter 9. It needs to be something they can track. If nothing else, have them write them down.
5. Day 6: Attitude. Describe ways to change their attitudes. This is an ongoing lesson that you should weave throughout all instruction.
6. Day 7: Revisit goals. Evaluate how they are doing while setting new ones. This could be done in just a few minutes, so it might not take a class period. Do this periodically.
7. Day 8: Credit score.

Appendix C

SMARTER Goals

	Questions to Ponder	Responses
Specific	What exactly do you want to accomplish?	
Measurable	How will you know when you have completed your goal? How will you measure your progress?	
Achievable	What knowledge do you need to ensure success?	
Relevant	Why is this important to you?	
Time-Bound	When will you complete this goal?	
Evaluate	When will you check in on your progress? How are you progressing?	
Re-adjust	What might you need to alter to accomplish this goal?	

Appendix D

What Is Your Passion Worksheet

What Is Your Passion...

...and how can you turn it into a career?

Take the time to ponder these questions. Then research and reflect upon the answers.

1. What do you enjoy doing?
2. What are you good at doing?
3. What do others say you are good at doing?
4. Are there any careers that combine these tangible things?
5. Do any of those careers interest you?
6. Pick one of those careers.
7. What education (formal or not) do you need to have to obtain this career?
8. Where can you get this education?
9. If it is not provided in a formal setting, then how will you obtain this career?
10. How much money will it cost to achieve this knowledge?
11. How much time will it cost?
12. How in demand is this career?
13. How much money can you make on the high and low end of this career?
14. Who is someone you can research who has succeeded in this career?
15. What other specific skills will you need to have to make it in this field? (Meaning soft skills like communication, teamwork, problem solving and so on.)
16. What is the likelihood you can obtain this as a career?

Appendix E

Handling Negativity and Credit

1. You have to be fully committed to change.
2. Check your anchors. Identify the emotion or evidence to which your attitude is anchored. Weigh out the pros and cons of the opportunity, and find a new place to anchor. (Essentially, reprogram your RAS to see the positive.)
3. In the short-term, fake an attitude change by changing how you move.
4. Be proactive. Prepare yourself for those events that trigger a bad attitude. Anticipate them. Then map out how you will handle them.
5. For the long term, you must alter what you are feeding your brain. Bad attitudes are toxic. Feed it good, positive food.

Ways to Handle Negative Feedback

1. If you know you are a sensitive person, then don't post anything, or at least turn off the replies.
2. Follow people you know. It is way more difficult to serve up that negativity to someone with whom you have a real, face-to-face relationship.
3. Before posting anything, anticipate the negative comments and plan how you will process them.
4. Remember, the faceless people commenting online most likely have low self-esteem and think poorly about themselves.
5. Pity them. They are drowning in a world of negativity. Misery loves company. Don't swim with them—that's what they want.
6. (You gotta say this next one while pumping your fists and banging on your chest.) Don't give them power or permission to hurt you!

How Do They Get a Credit Score?

A. Three companies gather the data.
B. Equifax, Experian, Transunion.
C. FICO, a separate company, interprets the data and assigns a score.

What Is a Credit Score Range?

For FICO it is 300–850

What Data Are They Gathering?

1. Payment History (35%)
2. Amount owed (30%)
3. Length of credit history (15%)
4. New credit (10%)
5. Type of credit used (10%)

Appendix F

The Mission

Planning a Mission Statement

1. In one sentence, what is the ONE message you want your students to understand by the end of the school year?
2. In one sentence, describe your classroom (not the physical layout).
3. When leaving your classroom at the end of the year, what do you want students to…

   …know?

   …feel?

   …say?
4. What value are you bringing to your students?
5. What NEW value do you bring to your classroom today?

Appendix G

Facets of Success Road Map and Easy Implementation

One of the best ways to truly track growth in an area is by setting up a Facets of Success chart. Below you will find steps to create your own chart.

1. To begin, hand draw or create this on a computer. It can include as many or as few facets as needed. Some common ones are: physical, emotional, friends, family, finances, education, and hobbies. They will be unique to each individual. You can include lines for half or even quarter numbers.

2. Design your scoring rubric for the categories. Try to make as much of the information as quantitative as possible. However, sometimes, you just can't quantify certain things, such as emotions. Therefore, you will need to use qualitative descriptive words.

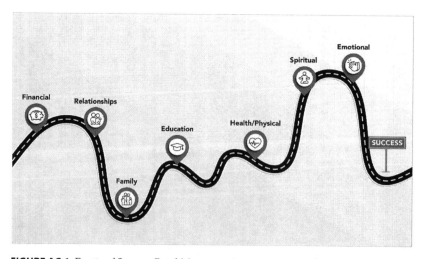

FIGURE AG.1 Facets of Success Road Map.

Facets of Success

FIGURE AG.2 Facets of Success.

This is an example of how a few of the categories/facets could be filled out. These are just examples. Be sure to make these your own. You will never enter the chart at a level five. If you do, then raise your standard. Enter the chart at a level two or three.

	Physical	*Emotional*	*Friends*	*Family*	*School*
1.	Exercise 3x Eat Right Feel Great	Conquering	Two friends who nourish and inspire you		
2.	Exercise 2x Good eating	Vibrant	One friend who nourishes and inspires you		
3.	Exercise 1x Improved diet	Good	Good friends, but not deep		
4.	Exercise 1x Poor diet	Sluggish	Acquaintances		
5.	Inactive Poor diet	Depressed	Tolerate		

Figure AG.3 is an example of a hand drawn chart. The sticky notes show the current level on the rubric where the student begins collecting data. Just a reminder, you should never start at a level five. If you do, raise your standard.

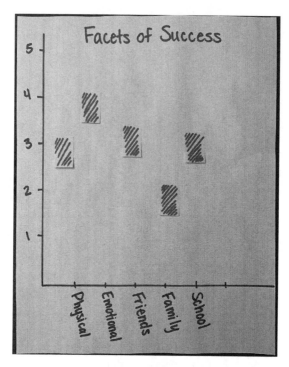

FIGURE AG.3 This is a quick hand drawn example of a facets of success chart.

3. Total your beginning numbers. They can be decimals if you like. On my chart, I total in quarter numbers. Record the date and total score of all the facets combined. For example: Total: 17 Date: 8/8/2022

4. Final step, periodically evaluate where you are on the chart. Raise your sticky note up or down accordingly. Once again, total your score. This is where it gets exciting, seeing how you are growing in each area. If you get them all up to a level 4, then create a new rubric. Continue to raise your standard!

Appendix H

Charting Facets of Success Lessons

This chart is an example of how you can track which classes have been taught the content.

2019-2020	Passion Discussion	Passion Research	Success Discussion	Success Reflection	Value Reflection	Other Three Legs	Motivation	Goal Setting	Goal Setting Two	Attitude	Attitude	Attitude	Attitude	Credit
0														
1														
2														
3														
4														
5														
6														
7														

FIGURE AH.1 Tracking Chart.